White-Collar Crime and Criminal Careers

Criminologists have turned their attention to the origins and paths of the criminal career for what this approach reveals about the causes, manifestations, and prevention of crime. Studies of the criminal career to date have focused on common criminals and street crime; criminologists have overlooked the careers of white-collar offenders. David Weisburd and Elin Waring offer here the first detailed examination of the criminal careers of people convicted of white-collar crimes.

Who are repeat white-collar criminals, and how do their careers differ from those of offenders found in more traditional crime samples? Weisburd and Waring uncover some surprising findings, which upset some long-held common wisdom about white-collar criminals. Most scholars, for example, have assumed that white-collar criminals, unlike other types of offenders, are unlikely to have multiple or long criminal records. As Weisburd and Waring demonstrate, a significant number of white-collar criminals have multiple contacts with the criminal justice system and like other criminals, they are often led by situational forces such as financial or family crises to commit crimes. White-collar criminals share a number of similarities in their social and economic circumstances with other types of criminals. Weisburd and Waring are led to a portrait of crimes and criminals that is very different from that which has traditionally dominated criminal career studies. It focuses less on the categorical distinctions between criminals and noncriminals and more on the importance of the immediate context of crime and its role in leading otherwise conventional people to violate the law.

David Weisburd is Professor of Criminology at Hebrew University Law School and Senior Research Fellow in the Department of Criminology and Criminal Justice at the University of Maryland in College Park.

Elin Waring is Associate Professor of Sociology at Lehman College and the Graduate Center, City University of New York.

Ellen F. Chayet is Production Director of Criminal Justice Press.

Cambridge Studies in Criminology

Editors
Alfred Blumstein, *H. John Heinz School of Public Policy and Management, Carnegie Mellon University*
David Farrington, *Institute of Criminology, University of Cambridge*

The Cambridge Studies in Criminology aims to publish the highest quality research on criminology and criminal justice topics. Typical volumes report major quantitative, qualitative, and ethnographic research, or make a substantial theoretical contribution. There is a particular emphasis on research monographs, but edited collections may also be published if they make an unusually distinctive offering to the literature. All relevant areas of criminology and criminal justice are to be included, for example, the causes of offending, juvenile justice, the development of offenders, measurement and analysis of crime, victimization research, policing, crime prevention, sentencing, imprisonment, probation, and parole. The series is global in outlook, with an emphasis on work that is comparative or holds significant implications for theory or policy.

Other books in the series:

White-Collar Crime
and Criminal Careers

David Weisburd   Elin Waring

With Ellen F. Chayet

CAMBRIDGE
UNIVERSITY PRESS

PUBLISHED BY THE PRESS SYNDICATE OF THE UNIVERSITY OF CAMBRIDGE
The Pitt Building, Trumpington Street, Cambridge, United Kingdom

CAMBRIDGE UNIVERSITY PRESS
The Edinburgh Building, Cambridge CB2 2RU, UK
40 West 20th Street, New York, NY 10011-4211, USA
10 Stamford Road, Oakleigh, VIC 3166, Australia
Ruiz de Alarcón 13, 28014 Madrid, Spain
Dock House, The Waterfront, Cape Town 8001, South Africa

http://www.cambridge.org

First published 2001

Printed in the United States of America

Typeface ITC New Baskerville 11/13 pt.   *System* QuarkXPress [BTS]

A catalog record for this book is available from the British Library.

Library of Congress Cataloging in Publication Data
Weisburd, David.
White-collar crime and criminal careers / David Weisburd, Elin
Waring.
p.   cm. – (Cambridge studies in criminology)
Includes bibliographical references and index.
ISBN 0-521-77162-5 – ISBN 0-521-77763-1 (pbk.)
1. White collar crimes.   2. Commercial criminals.   I. Waring, Elin J.
II. Title.   III. Series.
HV6768.W44   2001
364.16′8 – dc21   00-031260

ISBN 0 521 77162 5 hardback
ISBN 0 521 77763 1 paperback

For Sarit Esther, with respect for all she has accomplished and with love for who she is – D.W.

For Linnea and Bobby, with love – E.J.W.

For my husband, Bob; daughter, Amelia; father, Al; and the memory of my mother, Rebecca – E.F.C.

Contents

List of Figures

List of Tables

Acknowledgments

Having completed this book, we look back with great appreciation to all of those that have helped us along the way. At the very outset we owe a debt to Winnifred Reed of the National Institute of Justice. Not only did she have faith in our project and its importance, but she also worked tirelessly in helping us to gain the data we needed to develop our study. Without her efforts and those of the then director of the National Institute of Justice, Charles K. Stewart, our work would never have gotten under way. We owe special appreciation as well to Stanton Wheeler, our teacher and mentor, who introduced us to the problem of white-collar crime and initiated the original study from which our work developed. We were also aided in the early stages of our work by the advice of colleagues who helped us to become familiar with the idea of criminal careers and its application to a white-collar crime sample. While many provided thoughtful advice, we are particularly indebted to Jan Chaiken, now the Director of the Bureau of Justice Statistics, Jackie Cohen of Carnegie Mellon University, Richard Linster of the National Institute of Justice, and Michael Maltz of the University of Illinois. We owe a special debt to Michael Maltz, who also acted as statistical consultant on this project. Michael followed our work from the very outset to its completion, commenting not only on our analysis but also on the final drafts of our manuscript.

In the development of the database that forms the focus of our analyses, we relied upon many students. In this regard we were fortunate to have our research housed at the School of Criminal Justice at Rutgers University at a time when so many talented young people were pursuing their studies. Among those who helped us were George Clarke, Dory Dickman, Mary Brewster, Robin Lincoln, Robyn Mace, and Sue Plant. We want to acknowledge in particular the contributions of Sue Plant and Dory Dickman. They formed the backbone of our research team and spent many long hours ensuring the quality of the data collection process.

We were also aided by colleagues and students in the development of the manuscript. A special thanks goes to Phyllis Schultze, the criminal justice librarian at Rutgers University, who not only helped us find the sources we needed but also directed us to many of them. We are also indebted to Tamar Tomer, a doctoral student at the Hebrew University Law School, and Anne Mari McNally, a research associate at the Police Foundation, who worked tirelessly to make sure that we were up to date in identifying the work of others. Tamar also provided much general help in the development of drafts of our work. Support in the development of the manuscript was also provided by Sandra Wright, Heather Sparks, and Kelli Edwards.

We are very grateful as well to colleagues who took time from their other work to provide thoughtful comments on drafts of this book. We are especially indebted to the following individuals for their critical perspectives: Delbert Elliot of the University of Colorado; Orli Goldschmidt, Vered Vinitzky, Anat Horovitz, and Michael Beenstock of the Hebrew University; Bill Laufer of the University of Pennsylvania; Kip Schelegel of Indiana University; Neil Shover of the University of Tennessee; Rosann Greenspan of the Police Foundation; and Christy Visher of the National Institute of Justice. Two anonymous reviewers for Cambridge University Press also provided helpful comments.

We want to thank especially Albert Blumstein and David Farrington for their thoughtful review of our book, as well as their support in bringing it to publication. We also owe a debt to our editor, Mary Child, who not only believed in the idea of our book, but also read it carefully and forced us to make it a bit more accessible to the reader.

The funding for any research effort of this size is crucial, and we want to acknowledge our debt to the National Institute of Justice and its generous support for our work through grant 88-IJ-CX-0046. While we appreciate the support of the Institute, the opinions and positions expressed in this book are exclusively ours and do not necessarily represent the views of the National Institute of Justice or the U.S. Department of Justice.

Finally, we want to express our love and appreciation to Shelly and Tom, who suffered through our long hours and endured our many meetings and telephone calls. Without their support we would not have managed to complete this work.

David Weisburd
Elin Waring

White-Collar Crime and Criminal Careers

When Edwin Sutherland coined the term "white-collar crime" in his address to the American Sociological Society in 1939, he used the concept to challenge conventional stereotypes and theories.[1] In 1939, crime was generally seen as the work of disadvantaged young men from broken homes and decaying neighborhoods. Through films and books, the criminal was portrayed as a tough guy growing up on the wrong side of town. He was either to be saved by the church or the community or to be condemned to a sad fate determined by the difficult circumstances in which he was raised.

Such stereotypes were not limited to popular images of criminality. In a series of enduring empirical inquiries, sociologists at the University of Chicago in the 1920s and 1930s emphasized the link between social disorganization and poverty in areas within a city and high rates of criminal behavior (e.g., see Thrasher, 1927; Shaw, 1929). Their work, which continues to have an important place in American criminology (e.g., see Reiss and Tonry, 1986), served to focus attention on crimes of the lower classes. When Sutherland gave his ground-breaking speech to the American

---

[1] The address was published the following year in the *American Sociological Review* under the title "White Collar Criminality" (Sutherland, 1940).

Sociological Society, scholars and lay people alike saw poverty or conditions associated with poverty as intricately linked to criminality.

Sutherland challenged the traditional image of criminals and the predominant etiological theories of crime of his day. The white-collar criminals he identified were often middle-aged men of respectability and high social status. They lived in affluent neighborhoods, and they were well respected in the community. Sutherland was not the first to draw attention to such criminals. In earlier decades, scholars such as W.A. Bonger (1916) and E.A. Ross (1907) and popular writers such as Upton Sinclair (1906) and Lincoln Steffens (1903) pointed out a variety of misdeeds by businessmen and elites. However, such people were seldom considered by those who wrote about or studied crime and were not a major concern of the public or policy makers when addressing the crime problem.

Sutherland (1940) argued that the predominant conceptions and explanations of crime in his day were "misleading and incorrect" because they were developed from "biased samples" of criminals and criminal behavior (see also Sutherland, 1945, 1949). He noted that "vast areas of criminal behavior of persons not in the lower class" had been neglected in prior studies (1940, p. 2). In Sutherland's view, poverty and social disorganization could not be seen as the primary causes of crime, if crime could also be found among people who grew up in "good neighborhoods and good homes" and lived in situations of authority and privilege. He believed that much could be learned about the crime problem by focusing on the category of white-collar crime. He declared that white-collar crime was not an isolated phenomenon, but a significant part of the landscape of criminal behavior.

Despite Sutherland's recognition of the importance of the white-collar crime category, it never achieved the centrality in criminological study that he proposed. White-collar crime has for the most part been treated as a deviant case, invoked primarily to provide a contrast to the common crimes and street criminals that continue to dominate research and theory about crime. In this book, we seek to return the white-collar crime category to the mainstream of criminological thought. Our specific focus is on what criminologists term *criminal careers* (see Blumstein et al., 1982, 1986). Much research on crime has focused on general portraits of crime in the population. The concern of such studies is with aggregate crime rates in communities or regions of the country or the relative changes in crime rates over time. The criminal career approach, in contrast, "seeks to analyze the activity – the careers – of the individuals who commit criminal offenses" (Blumstein et al., 1986, p. 1). It directs attention to the factors that lead to participation in crime, the nature and seriousness of criminal behavior of active offenders, and the duration of their involvement. In this context, the criminal career approach allows scholars and policy makers to focus directly on the causes of criminality, and potential methods of effective prevention and treatment of crime (Farrington et al., 1986).

Though the study of criminal careers has come to occupy a central place in the study of crime, criminologists have largely overlooked the criminal careers of white-collar offenders. For study of criminal careers, as with study of other crime and justice problems, the primary focus of researchers has been upon street crimes and common criminals. The fact that white-collar criminals have been assumed to be one-shot offenders (e.g., see Edelhertz and Overcast, 1982; Wheeler, Mann, and Sarat, 1988) has reinforced this bias. Even though there is a long tradition of scholarship dating back to Sutherland (1949) that recognizes that white-collar criminals, like common criminals, may repeat their involvement in law violating acts, most scholars (including Sutherland) have assumed that white-collar criminals are unlikely to have multiple contacts with the criminal justice system. Because such contacts have formed an important part of the study of criminal careers (Blumstein et al., 1986), white-collar crime has not been seen as a fruitful area of concern for criminal career researchers.

Our study contradicts this common assumption about white-collar criminals. In the chapters that follow we show that a substantial number of offenders who are convicted under white-collar crime statutes in the United States federal courts have multiple contacts with the criminal justice system. This fact led us to explore the problem of white-collar criminal careers, allowing us to examine white-collar crimes and criminals using a different approach than has traditionally been applied by other white-collar crime scholars. It also provides us with an opportunity to critically examine assumptions about criminality and criminal careers that have been developed primarily in the context of studies of street criminals.

In taking this approach we are led to a portrait of crimes and criminals that is very different from that which has traditionally dominated criminology. Criminologists have generally focused on the ways in which criminals differ from those not involved in crime. As Thomas Gabor (1994, p. 14) writes:

> Traditionally, criminologists have attempted to explain why some people become criminals and others do not. Some have attributed the apparent differences between criminals and the law-abiding to innate or genetic factors, others to personality differences, and still others to social circumstances. Whatever their persuasion, these traditionalists shared the assumption that there were clear differences between criminals and the rest of society. The traditional goal of research and theory in criminology, therefore, has been to identify these differences as precisely as possible.

The emphasis that traditional scholarship has placed on distinguishing between criminals and noncriminals adds little to understanding the involvement in crime of many of those we study. Rather, our data suggest the importance of the immediate context of crime and its role in leading otherwise conventional people to violate the law.

White-Collar Crime and Criminal Careers

This book centers both on description of the criminal careers of white-collar offenders and on the implications that the study of white-collar criminal careers has for understanding criminality more generally. The fact that white-collar criminals, like common crime offenders, often have multiple contacts with the criminal justice system raises a number of intriguing questions. Who are these repeat white-collar criminals, and how are they different from white-collar offenders who have only one recorded contact with the criminal justice system? How are their criminal careers similar to or different from offenders found in more traditional crime samples?

It might be, for example, that repeat white-collar offenders, as defined by the criminal justice system, are similar to other white-collar criminals, but are just unlucky enough to be caught more than once. This would be consistent with research on corporate offending which suggests that such criminality is part of an established pattern of behavior for law violators (Clinard and Yeager, 1980; Braithwaite, 1982; Sutherland, 1949). On the other hand, some might argue that those convicted of white-collar crimes who have multiple contacts with the criminal justice system are not likely to be white-collar criminals at all. An example consistent with this argument would be a criminal who is a high-level manager of an illegal drug distribution network who was prosecuted for a white-collar crime, such as tax evasion, merely because other prosecutorial avenues were too difficult.

The occurrence of repeat criminality in a sample of offenders convicted of white-collar crimes also raises the issue of whether these offenders differ from street crime offenders in the basic parameters of their criminal careers. As we have already noted, white-collar offenders have generally been assumed to have infrequent contacts with the criminal justice system. In fact, do white-collar offenders have official criminal histories of much lower frequency than street crime offenders? Do they start and end their criminal careers later in the life course than do other types of offenders? If common stereotypes of white-collar offenders hold true, we would not expect to find that such criminals are active offenders early in life. However, we might expect that they would continue to reoffend much later in life than street crime offenders. This in turn would imply that the duration of criminal careers of white-collar offenders may be particularly long. Prior studies offer little insight into these concerns.

The question of specialization is particularly important in the study of white-collar criminal careers. Does it make sense, for example, to speak of "white-collar criminals" if such offenders are likely to engage in common criminal behavior as well as white-collar criminality? It would certainly alter the prevailing image of white-collar crime if white-collar offenders were found, for example, to commit more serious violent crimes at other points in their criminal careers.

The study of white-collar crime and criminal careers offers a special opportunity for critically examining the appropriateness of the concept of career for understanding the development of criminal activities among offenders. Unlike most street criminals, white-collar offenders are often employed and may have conventional career histories. How does criminality intersect with those careers, and to what extent does it appear to be an important part of their development? Similarly, does repeat criminality among white-collar criminals provide evidence of systematic development of paths to crime, or does it suggest a series of random and chance events that are a small part of the life course?

What of the relationship between the social backgrounds and histories of offenders and involvement in crime on the one hand, and the relevance of situational characteristics of crime on the other? Does involvement in crime appear to be related to characteristics that are common to white-collar criminals but not others in similar social and economic circumstances? Does the criminality of white-collar offenders appear as a natural outcome of a life that is typified by deviance more generally? Or conversely, does it appear for these offenders that "opportunity makes the thief" (Felson and Clarke, 1998) – that white-collar criminals are conventional people who confront specific situational opportunities that lead them to crime? Or must we distinguish among different types of offenders who commit white-collar crime?

Some criminologists argue that it is essential to examine very specific categories of crime and deviance, such as car theft or house-hold burglary, rather than overarching groupings such as white-collar crime, because there may be important differences between them (Clarke, 1980, 1983, 1992, 1995; Clarke and Cornish, 1985). Thus, we might find very different pathways leading to involvement in crime among different types of offenders in our sample. Are such differences related to the types of crime that offenders commit or to the frequency of offending? What can we learn more generally about crime and criminality from the different types of offenders identified in a white-collar crime sample?

At least since the time Sutherland began his study of white-collar criminals there has been concern that high-status offenders avoid the most severe sanctions in the justice system (Wheeler et al., 1982; Meier and Short, 1982; Clinard and Yeager, 1980; Watkins, 1977). In recent years, such concerns have led in the federal sentencing system to increased severity in the penalties for white-collar crimes (U.S. Sentencing Commission, 1987) and to a much larger number of such offenders being sentenced to imprisonment (U.S. Sentencing Commission, 1991). For the most part, these policies have been developed without an understanding of how these changes will impact the potential for future criminal conduct among sanctioned white-collar criminals. Do criminal sanctions decrease the likelihood of reoffending, or the timing or seriousness of reoffending, of those convicted of white-collar crimes? Or do criminal sanctions "backfire" (Farrington et al., 1986; Sherman et al., 1986; Petersilia and Turner, 1986; Bridges and Stone, 1986) in a white-collar crime sample and lead to more serious involvement in crime? Finally, do different types of sanctions – for example, prison or fines – have distinct types of influences on the criminal careers of convicted white-collar criminals?

Defining White-Collar Crime and Sampling White-Collar Criminals

In order to provide insight into these questions, we sought to carefully examine the social and criminal histories of a sample of white-collar offenders. We recognize at the outset, however, that our view of white-collar crime and criminal careers is strongly influenced by the nature of the white-collar criminals we study. Therefore, we now focus in detail on our approach to the problem of white-collar crime and the sample of white-collar offenders that we study.

Defining White-Collar Crime

The absence of a precise definition of white-collar crime has plagued white-collar crime scholars from the outset (Schlegel and

Weisburd, 1992). The confusion began with Sutherland himself (Geis, 1992; Coleman, 1992; Wheeler, 1983). Sometimes he stressed crimes committed by individuals of high status, while at other times he stressed crimes carried out in the course of one's occupation (e.g., see Sutherland, 1939, 1945). In his major empirical contribution to study of white collar crime, he focused on crimes committed by organizations or by individuals acting in organizational capacities (Sutherland, 1949). Although he used various definitions, the most frequently cited definition draws attention both to the established social standing of white-collar criminals and to the special opportunities for crime that come from specific occupational positions. He wrote: "White-collar crime may be defined approximately as a crime committed by a person of respectability and high social status in the course of his occupation" (Sutherland, 1949, p. 9).

Sutherland's definition established status, occupation, and organization as central features of white-collar crime study. However, in the more than half century since he coined the term, it has come to have different meanings depending on the research problem encountered or the theoretical context explored. For some, the concept is centered squarely in the activities of the most elite and powerful members of society. For example, Geis (1992, p. 47) argues that white-collar crime involves the "abuse of power by persons who are situated in high places where they are provided with the opportunity for such abuse." For others, white-collar crime refers not to the social positions of offenders but rather to the context in which white-collar crimes are carried out or to the methods used in their commission. This latter approach is reflected in early studies of occupational crime, such as Earl Quinney's (1963) examination of prescription violations by retail pharmacists, or Frank Hartung's (1950) study of violations of wartime regulations in the meat industry (see also Newman, 1958). It is also reflected in Herbert Edelhertz's influential definition of white-collar crime, as "an illegal act or series of illegal acts committed by nonphysical means and by concealment or guile, to obtain money or property, to avoid the payment or loss of money or property, or to obtain business or personal advantage" (Edelhertz, 1970, p. 3).

While an array of definitions of white-collar crime has been offered since Sutherland coined the term (see also Reiss and Biderman, 1980; Shapiro, 1990), they have in common an underlying theme that is linked to Sutherland's original interest in the concept. Whatever the definition proposed, scholars have tried to define a category of crimes and criminals that provides a clear contrast to the common crimes and street criminals that generally attract the attentions of lay people and scholars. High social status is not a trait that is normally associated with crime, nor indeed is white-collar occupational status. Street criminals often use guns or knives to steal from their victims, they do not rely on paper instruments or computers as methods for committing their offenses. In some basic sense, the different definitions of white-collar crime intersect one with another. People of higher social status are those most likely to have white-collar occupational position, and such people are more likely to have the opportunity to commit crimes that involve nonphysical means. The question, however, is how broad the boundaries of white-collar crime study should be. While the differing definitions have much in common, they draw the dividing line between white-collar and other crime in different places.

Debate over the boundaries of white-collar crime study has gained new intensity as a result of a series of empirical studies that examine the types of people that are prosecuted for what are ordinarily defined as white-collar crimes. These studies suggest that much of what has been assumed to be white-collar crime is committed by people in the middle rather than upper classes of our society (e.g., see Croall, 1989; Levi, 1987; Weisburd et al., 1991). Many of the "fraudsters" who manipulate stocks are very far from elite status. Most of those who are prosecuted for crimes like bribery, tax fraud, or bank fraud are rather average in their social backgrounds and positions. The predominance of the more ordinary type of white-collar offender may be, to some extent, a function of the vagaries of prosecution rather than the realities of offending. Nonetheless, it is not a trivial fact that most of those prosecuted for so-called white-collar crimes have little in common with the powerful and wealthy individuals who are often conjured up as images of the typical white-collar offender. However, it is also important that they differ at least as sharply from the lower-class criminals that are generally thought of when scholars or lay people discuss the crime problem.

These white-collar criminals differ in status and position from more elite white-collar offenders, and their crimes are frequently as mundane as their social backgrounds. But it would be misleading to overstate the differences in their opportunities to commit costly and complex white-collar illegalities. It is not necessary to be a Fortune 500 corporate executive to develop a costly stock or land fraud. Such crimes are often committed in small firms or by employees who hold less powerful positions in larger ones. Antitrust violations involving millions of dollars are often committed by local businessmen or women. Frauds netting millions of dollars are frequently perpetrated by middle-level bureaucrats in public and private agencies who have access to large sums of money through government aid programs.

Should these middle-class white-collar criminals be included within the boundaries of white-collar crime study? Some scholars have suggested that such offenders are a useful subject of inquiry, but that they are too far afield from Sutherland's original conception to add much to our understanding of the problem of white-collar crime (e.g., see Geis, 1992; Shover, 1999). The question is whether it is useful to begin with an understanding of white-collar crime that allows us to speak not only of the rich and powerful white-collar criminals, but also of those offenders much closer to the middle of our society who have recently become the subject of scholarly attention. A simple response to this question would note that were we to narrow the scope of white-collar crime research to the most elite white-collar criminals, we would exclude the bulk of those people who are convicted for so-called white-collar crimes. Though from the outset scholars have contended that white-collar criminals often escape detection and prosecution, it seems unreasonable to us to argue that most offenders who are prosecuted for white-collar crimes should be excluded from systematic study.

Beyond this we believe that Sutherland's emphasis on elite status was in part a function of the different opportunity structure for white-collar criminality that existed in his day.[2] It was natural for Sutherland to focus on businessmen in lofty positions when examining the problem of white-collar crime because relatively few Americans beyond these elite men had any opportunity for committing such illegalities. But changes in our society since then have placed the opportunity for white-collar crimes in the hands of a much broader class of Americans, most of them people who were excluded from these activities in the past. In part, the rapid growth of white-collar jobs in America in the last fifty years has spawned such changes (Bell, 1973). But perhaps even more important are the dramatic differences in the way modern society functions. The advent of the computer, for example, gives large numbers of people access to the documents and transactions that are so much a part of white-collar illegalities. The growth of modern state bureaucracies has placed millions of dollars in the hands of people who would never have had access to such sums in the past.[3] The development of a credit economy has also expanded the opportunities for such crimes.

A Broad and Heterogeneous Sample of White-Collar Offenders

The sample we use for studying white-collar criminal careers takes this more inclusive approach to the problem of white-collar crime. It was designed to identify the broad range of white-collar crimes and criminals prosecuted in American federal courts. The sample was originally selected by researchers at Yale Law School working under the leadership of Stanton Wheeler (see Wheeler, Weisburd, and Bode, 1988; Weisburd et al., 1991). We benefit from the

[2] For a more in-depth discussion of these issues see Weisburd et al., 1991, Chapter 7.

[3] As federal programs have expanded over a wider range of activities, the federal government has become the source of financing for a wide variety of purposes. As Weisburd et al. (1991, p. 11) note, "this has led to the use of government programs as a locus for the commission of financial fraud." While the sums involved in such crimes may be large, the perpetrators are often middle-class people, many times owners of small businesses (Weisburd et al., 1991).

careful sampling techniques and rich data collected in that study. At the same time, we add detailed information on the number, timing, and types of other criminal events attributed to these offenders both before and after the offense that was the focus of the Yale study. Because our sample is drawn from the Yale Law School study, we describe below the approach used by Wheeler and his colleagues to identify their sample and the data collected.

White-collar crime was defined by Wheeler, Weisburd, and Bode (1982, p. 642; see also Shapiro, 1981) as "economic offenses committed through the use of some combination of fraud, deception, or collusion." They examined eight federal crimes that fit, in their statutory descriptions, this broad definition: antitrust offenses, securities fraud, mail and wire fraud, false claims and statements, credit and lending institution fraud, bank embezzlement, income tax fraud, and bribery.[4] The sample was selected with the intent of providing "a broad and heterogeneous view of the white-collar criminal activity that is prosecuted in the Federal Courts" (Weisburd et al., 1991, p. 11). The Yale researchers noted that they identified crime categories "that would most frequently be identified by persons as 'presumptively' white-collar" (Wheeler et al., 1982, p. 643).

The original sample was drawn primarily from cases processed in seven federal judicial districts during fiscal years 1976–1978. The districts were chosen in part to provide geographic spread, in part because they were being examined in other studies, and in part because some of them were known to have a substantial amount of white-collar crime prosecution. The districts (and their central cities) are: Central California (Los Angeles), Northern Georgia (Atlanta), Northern Illinois (Chicago), Maryland (Balti-

---

[4] For a description of the statutory categories examined see Appendix A. The titles and sections of the main statutes examined are: Antitrust, 15 USC 1-3; Securities, 15 USC 77-78; Mail and Wire Fraud, 18 USC 1341 and 18 USC 1343; False Claims and Statements, 18 USC 287 and 18 USC 1001; Credit and Lending Institution Fraud, 18 USC 1014; Bank Embezzlement, 18 USC 656; Income Tax Fraud, 26 USC 7201, 26 USC 7203, and 26 USC 7206; Bribery, 18 USC 201.

more), Southern New York (Manhattan and the Bronx), Northern Texas (Dallas), and Western Washington (Seattle).

A stratified random sample of a maximum of thirty convicted defendants was selected from each offense category in each of these seven districts.[5] The sample was stratified to allow a sufficient number of cases of relatively less common, but theoretically important, white-collar crimes such as bribery, antitrust offenses, and securities frauds.[6] A supplementary sample of securities and antitrust offenders was also collected. This supplementary sample included all offenders convicted of these crimes during the three-year sample period from all United States federal judicial districts. In this and subsequent chapters we refer to the crime that led to selection into the sample as the "criterion" offense.

The database compiled in the original research was created with specific information about offenders drawn from presentence investigation reports (PSIs). Like other matters of systematic criminal record keeping, PSIs are routinely filled out for those

---

[5] For specific offenses in specific districts, thirty cases were not available for sampling. In this situation the Yale researchers included all available offenders in the sample. See Appendix A for a description of the sampling frame.

[6] The sample thus includes more securities, antitrust, and bribery cases and fewer bank embezzlement and mail and wire fraud cases than would be expected from a simple random sample. However, oversampling resulting from stratification was constrained by the fact that rarer offenses often did not meet the sampling threshold (see footnote 5). This is illustrated by comparing the distribution of offenses in the sample with that in the national population of cases in 1978 (the first year that the Federal Judicial Center reports separate out felony from other cases). Caution should be used in the case of antitrust offenses, because many corporate offenders are included in the Federal Judicial Center statistics: [S – sample; P – national population] Bribery S – 7.7% P – 3.1%; Income Tax S – 19.2% P – 17.9%; Bank Embezzlement S – 18.3% P – 21.3%; Credit and Lending Institution Fraud S – 14.4% P – 9.6%; False Claims and Statements S – 14.4% P – 15.2%; Mail and Wire Fraud S – 17.4% P – 26.4%; Securities Fraud S – 6.1% P – 2.8%; Antitrust S – 2.5% P – 3.5%.

who pass a certain threshold in the criminal justice system, namely, conviction in a federal court. At the time of the study, presentence reports provided a particularly rich source of information not only on the nature of the crimes committed but also for understanding the offenders prosecuted. Before a major change in the Rules of Criminal Procedure that eliminated or minimized much of the social history information in the PSIs went into effect in 1987 (see Findley and Ross, 1989), the report was required to include "any prior criminal record of the defendant, information about his characteristics and financial condition, information about circumstances affecting his behavior, and any other information required by the court" (Fennell and Hall, 1980).

A sense for the comprehensive nature of the document can be gained from Fennell and Hall's description of preparation of presentence investigations at that time (Fennell and Hall, 1980, pp. 1623–1625):

> The line probation officer traditionally starts the presentence investigation by conducting an in-depth interview with the defendant at the probation office. In this interview, the officer attempts to establish a cooperative relationship with the defendant to obtain the defendant's version of the offense and arrest as well as all other relevant information. After the interview, the probation officer contacts the United States Attorney and the investigating agents involved in the case to obtain their version of the offense. These inquiries often uncover additional information about the defendant's activities that goes beyond the scope of the instant offense.
>
> . . . Insight into the defendant's social stability is sought by contacting social service agencies with which the defendant has dealt, present and former employers, family members and indviduals in the community who may know the defendant. The officer also has access to any recorded contacts the defendant has had with the military, law enforcement authorities, educational institutions, banks and credit bureaus. Finally, the probation officer obtains available medical and clinical evaluations of the defendant's mental and physical health. After most of this information is obtained, the probation officer reinterviews the defendant in the

defendant's home, with the hope that the defendant will be more candid in a familiar setting. At this time, the probation officer usually confronts the defendant with any information that differs substantially from his original statements, and attempts to resolve the discrepancies.

The fact that the PSIs were subject to challenge by both defense and prosecution suggests that the "facts" provided are often reliable.[7] Nonetheless, a number of legal scholars had criticized the format of PSIs during the period these data were collected because the information included often did not meet the evidentiary standards generally required in legal proceedings (e.g., see *Yale Law Journal*, 1982). Sometimes the probation officers reported unsubstantiated rumors and hearsay, and the information included is, of course, filtered through the eyes of the probation officers themselves. While the wide range of information collected in the presentence investigations raised important procedural and legal concerns, the availability of the PSIs (ordinarily not provided to researchers at that time) allowed Yale researchers to develop an unusually detailed data base on the criminals they studied. Our access to these data, as well as the PSIs from which they are drawn, provided us with a rich source from which to begin our investigation into white-collar criminal careers.

While the sample was carefully devised and the data source unusually detailed, it is necessarily limited in some respects (see Weisburd et al., 1991, pp. 17–20). The selection of cases draws offenders who have been prosecuted for felony offenses in federal courts. Accordingly, white-collar offenders who have only been prosecuted in state courts or those who have been prosecuted only under administrative or civil law are not included in the sample. The sample is also drawn from a population of convicted

---

[7] Nonetheless, Fennell and Hall (1980) report that in practice the reports were often not shared with the defense. Moreover, we recognize that in going beyond reporting of "facts" about the offense or the offender's background, one can be much less sure of the PSIs accuracy.

defendants. This means that we also did not study white-collar offenders who had fallen under suspicion but had never been indicted and successfully prosecuted.[8]

We think that the choice of federal courts as a hunting ground for white-collar criminals was a good one, because it is generally recognized that white-collar crimes constitute a much larger proportion of prosecutions there than in state or local courts. However, the exclusion of civil and administrative violations as criteria for sampling and the inclusion of only convicted defendants raises more substantive concerns. How is our portrait of white-collar criminals biased by the failure to include offenders prosecuted for administrative or civil law violations, or those prosecuted for crimes but not found guilty?

There is evidence that those who are highest up the organizational and status hierarchies are somewhat less likely to be criminally prosecuted for white-collar crimes (e.g., see Shapiro, 1984, 1985). This would suggest that the sample is less likely to include the most elite white-collar crime offenders than would a sample that was drawn from a universe of civil and administrative law violators. But this bias should not be overstated. Those who observed prosecutors during the late 1970s and early 1980s found that they were more likely to target more serious crimes for criminal prosecution and that offenders of higher status were more likely to commit such crimes in the first place (Benson et al., 1988; Shapiro, 1985).

---

[8] There are also a number of other federal white-collar offenses that arguably might have been included in selecting a broad-based sample of white-collar crime. Perjury, bankruptcy fraud, and conspiracy are examples of these. Yale law school researchers excluded these, as well as other crime categories, in defining the sample because they were seen as "deficient" in one respect or another (Weisburd et al., 1991, p. 18). For example, it was suspected that perjury was used often to prosecute organized crime figures, conspiracy was most often a secondary crime and thus was already included in many cases, and crimes like bankruptcy fraud were prosecuted rarely in the districts studied. The sample also does not draw environmental or occupational safety and health violations, because these for the most part became criminal offenses only after the sample was selected.

What of the impact of the inclusion of only those who had been successfully prosecuted? Some who have studied white-collar crime prosecution have suggested that powerful business defendants are able to intervene and to delay enforcement efforts (e.g., see Coleman, 1989). Others argue that the professional aspirations of prosecutors may lead them to be more aggressive against more substantial white-collar crime cases (e.g., see Katz, 1979; Benson et al., 1988), which generally include more elite and powerful defendants (Weisburd et al., 1991). According to Kenneth Mann (1985), who conducted a study of the white-collar crime defense bar at the time these data were collected, the underlying criminal conduct of white-collar crime defendants in the cases that lead to conviction is often similar to the conduct of those who go free. The differences lie mainly in the vagaries of the evidentiary traces that are left behind; these traces enable some cases to be successfully prosecuted and others not.

Despite the limitations that we have described, this sample provides a unique opportunity for examining the social and criminal careers of a broad range of white-collar offenders. At the same time, it is important to note at the outset that the white-collar crimes included in the sample have a much more mundane quality than is often associated with white-collar crime in the popular imagination or in academic studies that focus on the most consequential white-collar crime cases. While the sample contains many examples of offenders who commit dramatic and complex frauds, the large majority of the white-collar crimes, including many of those committed by those of the highest status, are undramatic, and similar crimes could be committed by people of relatively modest social status.[9] These offenses differ systematically from common crimes (Weisburd et al., 1991). Nonetheless, they often have a common, everyday character. As Weisburd et al. (1991, p. 171) note:

> Their basic ingredients are lying, cheating, and fraud, and for every truly complicated and rarified offense there are many others that are simple, and could be carried out by almost anyone who can read, write and give an outward appearance of stability. The

[9] See Weisburd et al. (1991, pp. 62–73).

offenders that got the most notoriety in Sutherland's day were Ivar Krueger and Samuel Insull, while today's most noted defendants are Ivan Boesky and Michael Milken. But now, just as in Sutherland's day, these cases are the exception, not the rule. If one wants to understand the full range of white-collar crime offending, one has to look beyond the most dramatic cases.

Tracking Criminal Careers

The original Yale database did not include detailed information on the nature or form of the offenders' criminal histories. Reflecting what was believed about white-collar criminals – that they were likely to have little or no official history of prior offending – the researchers decided to collect only very general information on criminal histories, such as the total number of arrests or most serious prior crime reported. However, when the research was complete, it was clear that the offenders studied had, on average, much more serious criminal records than had been expected (Weisburd et al., 1991, p. 66):

> . . . we should stress here that these white-collar criminals evidence prior criminality to a much greater extent than most practitioners and scholars would have expected. . . . Indeed as a group they are approximately twice as likely to have an arrest record as is the national population.

Over forty percent of the sample had a prior arrest reported in the PSIs, and more than one-third had a prior conviction. These results were not a fluke of the particular sample identified. Benson and Moore (1992) report very similar results for a study of white-collar crime in eight different federal judicial districts. They found that almost forty percent of white-collar offenders (including those convicted of bribery, bank embezzlement, income tax evasion, false claims and statements, and mail fraud) had prior arrests reported in their presentence investigations.

We sought both to gain more reliable data on prior criminality and to extend our view of criminal histories more than ten years beyond the "criterion offense" that had originally identified sample members.[10] The first critical decision in developing such information was the choice of a measure of criminality. We decided at the outset that it was impractical to collect self-report measures, though these had the potential to add significantly to our understanding of paths to crime for white-collar criminals. It was unlikely that, after such a long period of time, we would be able to track down a very large proportion of the original sample based on information available in the presentence investigations. Moreover, because our interest was in documenting criminal involvement, we felt that many individuals would be unable to accurately recollect the specific timing of criminal activities that had occurred many years in the past. Of course, this assumes that they would be cooperative in providing such information in the first place.[11]

Turning to official measures of criminality, we decided to focus on arrests for two main reasons. First, although we cannot determine when actual criminal behavior occurs, the best measure is generally one which comes closest in time to offending (Maltz, 1984). Second, although all measures of criminality include a substantial degree of error, that of a false positive (including some events as crimes that are not instances of offending) is generally considered to be less serious than that of a false negative (excluding some events as crimes because of attrition in criminal justice processing from arrest to conviction) (Maltz, 1984; Blumstein et al., 1986). Arrests are closer in time to the actual criminal events than other official measures of offending. Using arrests as an

---

[10] Because the sample includes offenders convicted over a three-year period, the follow-up time for each offender varies. Nonetheless, we have at a minimum a 126-month potential follow-up period (the actual follow-up period may be affected by the defendant's death; see p. 23) for all subjects in the study. With the exception of "time to failure" analyses in Chapters 5 and 6, we use a fixed follow-up period of 126 months in our analyses.

[11] Our reliance on official histories, rather than on self-reported activities, means that we also lack information on the offenders' personal histories over time including, for example, such items as changes in marital status following completion of the PSI.

official indicator of criminal behavior, we are, in turn, less likely to exclude potential crimes from our investigation.

While we believe that an arrest provides the best official measure of criminality, we recognize that it may be misleading at times to use arrests as indicators of the underlying criminal behavior of offenders or even the underlying patterns of criminal careers (see Kitsuse and Ciciourel, 1963; Wheeler, 1967; Elliott, 1995). Many offenders never get caught, and others get caught at different rates; for example, there are generally different estimates given of the relationship between recorded arrests and actual offenses depending on the type of offense examined (Blumstein et al., 1986). Despite these concerns, much of the research on the criminal careers of street criminals has been based on use of official data such as arrests (Elliott, 1995). As we seek to contrast this white-collar crime sample with more traditional studies, we deem arrest data particularly relevant. Moreover, our access to the presentence investigations allows us (as we describe later) to compare the official reports of criminality with the probation officers' interviews and overall assessment of the offenders studied.

Of course, a major concern in comparing arrests in this white-collar crime sample with arrests in other samples is whether they measure similar phenomena. It may be, for example, that the meaning of an arrest for a white-collar crime is different than that for a street crime. Prosecutors, not the police, are usually the primary investigators of white-collar crime (Katz, 1979). White-collar criminals may also be "arrested" much later in the investigative process than are street criminals, often because white-collar crimes are more difficult to unravel and many times do not have identifiable victims (Braithwaite and Geis, 1982). Such offenders may not be arrested at all if prosecutors decide to use civil actions instead of a criminal prosecution (Mann, 1992). We might, therefore, expect official records to underestimate the frequency of white-collar crime events in an offender's criminal career more seriously than is the case for common criminals (see Horney and Marshall, 1992).

Moreover, the fact that white-collar crimes generally are of longer duration than street crimes increases the potential for misunderstanding criminal careers in a sample of white-collar offenders (see Weisburd et al., 1991). For example, a land scheme that continues over several years may produce only one arrest. This certainly represents a much longer period of active criminality than does a single arrest for a theft or mugging or even one very active year in the history of a common crime offender in which dozens of offenses are committed. Accordingly, we might speculate that large gaps between officially reported crimes in a white-collar criminal career do not necessarily mean that such offenders are inactive during these periods.

Of course, this argument assumes that repeat white-collar criminals specialize to some degree in white-collar crime, a view that we challenge in later chapters. Furthermore, as noted above, white-collar crimes prosecuted in the federal courts generally do not approximate the complex, long-term offenses reported in the popular press. We suspect that the degree of bias created by using arrests to examine criminal histories in this sample may not be very different from that in other criminal populations. Nonetheless, the potential bias represented here is one that the reader should keep in mind when interpreting our study results.

Once arrest was defined as our primary measure of criminal history, it was natural that we attempt to gain access to Federal Bureau of Investigation "rap sheets." The rap sheet is generally considered the best single source of information on an individual's arrest history (Belair, 1985). It includes arrests from all jurisdictions in the United States and is routinely used by criminal justice agencies to identify and assess criminal records of offenders. In theory, the rap sheet also contains complete information on charges, dispositions, sanctions imposed and sentences served. These data, however, are not as reliably recorded as arrests (see Cooper et al., 1979; Belair, 1985).[12]

---

[12] A round table on data quality advised that dispositions are seriously underreported to the FBI, with estimates of between 30 percent and 50 percent of dispositions not reported. Arrests are apparently reported more reliably, although there is the potential for both underreporting and overreporting arrests. Both arrest and disposition information that is present is believed to be fairly accurate (see Belair, 1985).

While FBI rap sheets were not generally accessible to researchers at the time we collected our data, we were given access to these files because our study was funded by the National Institute of Justice.[13] But even with the full cooperation of the staff of the Identification Bureau of the FBI, we were not able to locate rap sheets for nearly three in ten of the offenders in the original Yale white-collar crime sample. Overall, the characteristics of cases with or without identifiable rap sheets are very similar.[14]

The FBI Identification Bureau informed us at the outset of our study that individuals who have died are purged from FBI criminal history databases. However, the FBI is alerted to death only when a Medical Examiner's office reports deaths to the FBI. Given the potential for confusing death with desistance from criminal-

---

[13] We owe a debt to Winifred Reed, the program manager for our study, and Charles Stewart, then Director of the National Institute of Justice, for their efforts in helping us gain access to the rap sheets.

[14] The inconsistency of retrieval of rap sheets was partly a function of the timing of our study, the timing of the original study, the age of our offenders, and the process of computerization of records at the FBI. The original study took place before FBI criminal history records were computerized. Because of their age, many of the offenders in our sample were low in the priority for the retrospective computerization that was in progress at the time of the current study.

While the sample overall is similar in characteristics to that selected by Wheeler et al. (1988), there are some differences. For example, in some districts offenders were less likely to have FBI identification numbers assigned prior to sentencing. In these cases we had to rely on name or other identifiers that were less likely to lead to successful matches. We were also less likely to receive rap sheets for older offenders, reflecting in part the Identification Bureau's practice of deleting files when a person reaches age 80. Nonetheless, the fact that we did receive several files on people over 80 suggests that such practices are often inconsistent. Those with more prior arrests in the original study were somewhat more likely to have identifiable rap sheets as were those who received an imprisonment sanction for the original offense. Women were, in turn, somewhat less likely to receive a rap sheet than men. While we note these differences, we do not believe that they have substantive impact on the findings reported in later chapters.

ity in a criminal career study, we sought to collect accurate information on mortality in the sample using a noncriminal justice data source.

The importance of identifying who in the sample had died and when death occurred was confirmed when we examined data drawn from the National Death Index.[15] In total, some fourteen percent of the cases for which we had a rap sheet had died between date of sentencing for the criterion offense and April 1990, the "censoring" date of our study or the date when our tracking of criminal histories ends. A similar proportion of those offenders for whom rap sheets were not received had also died by this date.

White-Collar Criminals: A Statistical Portrait of the Sample

Who are the white-collar criminals we study? While details about the crimes and criminals in our analyses are provided in subsequent chapters, it is useful to begin with a basic statistical portrait of the offenders in our sample. Generally, the sample is drawn from a very different population of convicted criminals than are samples of street crime offenders. For example, only nine percent of the sample as a whole was unemployed at the time the criterion offense was committed. This is a stark contrast to street criminals, most of whom are not employed in legitimate occupations (Sviridoff and McElroy, 1985). Similarly, the large majority of those working (90%) had white-collar jobs (as defined by the Census Bureau), and almost one-third of the sample were owners of or officers in businesses.

While the sample is clearly more "white collar" than a sample of street criminals would be, there is considerable variation in the background characteristics of those studied. This is illustrated when we examine the social and demographic characteristics of

[15] The National Death Index (NDI) is a centralized listing of a set of identifying information on all decedents whose deaths have been registered with the states since 1979 (Department of Health and Human Services, 1981).

offenders within each of the criterion offense categories used for selecting individuals for the sample (see Table 1.1). The eight legal categories cluster into four offender groupings.[16] At the top are antitrust and securities fraud offenders: generally middle-aged white males with stable employment in white-collar jobs and, more often than not, owners or officers in their companies. The antitrust offenders tend to be richer and are more likely to be college graduates.

The tax and bribery perpetrators are also predominantly white males, although a little more often unemployed and less well educated than their antitrust and securities fraud counterparts. At the same time they are generally steadily employed in white-collar jobs, and almost one-third are owners or officers in their businesses.

At the lower end of the spectrum are the credit fraud, false claims and mail fraud offenders. Fewer than half are steadily employed, and between fifteen and twenty percent of each category are unemployed at the time of their offenses. Compared with tax and bribery offenders, they are, on average, less likely to have substantial financial assets or to own their businesses. These offenders are younger, on average, than the others, and they are more likely to be female or "nonwhite,"[17] although white males continue to comprise the modal category.

Finally we have the bank embezzlers, who cannot be easily subsumed under one of these other three groups (though they are much closer to the bottom of the hierarchy than the top). They are far younger, on average, than the other offenders and are nearly as likely to be female as male. They are similar to the lowest of the three groups in financial assets, but they are far less likely than those offenders to be unemployed.

There is no one general profile of the offenders in our sample. There are several broad patterns, but there is also substantial vari-

---

[16] Our discussion here follows that of Weisburd et al. (1991, pp. 48–60). The sample described however, includes only those individuals for whom rap sheets were received.

[17] Nonwhites include those identified as "Negro," "American Indian," "Asian," and "Hispanic" on the PSI cover sheet. Nonwhites in this sample were predominantly African Americans.

Table 1.1. *A statistical portrait of the sample* (by the criterion offense)

	High		Middle		Low			
	Antitrust	SEC	Tax	Bribery	Credit fraud	False claims	Mail fraud	Bank embezzlement
Demographic characteristics								
Race (Percent white)	100.0%	99.4%	90.9%	79.3%	71.4%	58.0%	78.5%	74.2%
Sex (Percent male)	100.0%	99.4%	97.2%	94.3%	83.2%	84.0%	81.7%	53.4%
Age (Mean age)	50	44	45	42	37	38	37	30
Employment								
Percent steadily employed[a]	94.8%	59.3%	79.1%	63.8%	44.1%	39.6%	48.0%	34.2%
Percent employed in white-collar occupations[b]	96.4%	100.0%	77.6%	80.9%	88.4%	80.5%	84.9%	97.5%
Percent unemployed	0.0%	2.0%	6.0%	10.2%	14.4%	20.4%	17.0%	1.2%
Social class: Percent owners or officers	72.4%	68.2%	31.5%	28.3%	33.6%	12.6%	27.2%	14.7%
Personal history								
Financial standing								
Median assets	$145,500	$59,000	$45,500	$32,000	$6,500	$3,000	$2,000	$2,000
Median liabilities	$32,000	$58,000	$29,000	$19,000	$7,000	$3,000	$3,500	$3,000
Percent with college degree	50.0%	39.4%	23.4%	22.6%	21.0%	26.5%	23.9%	13.5%
Percent home owners	87.8%	61.4%	55.9%	44.0%	44.4%	37.0%	33.1%	31.8%
Percent married	93.1%	80.0%	64.4%	58.5%	47.9%	47.1%	49.4%	49.7%

[a] This variable refers to the five years preceding the PSI. Categories coded were: steady employment (or student), regular employment with some periods of unemployment, worked about half of the time, regular unemployment with periods of employment, steady unemployment, and inappropriate (e.g., the offender was retired for the whole five years). Percents are calculated using the whole sample for whom information was available.

[b] This uses standard Census Bureau classification of occupations and consists mainly of managers and professionals (e.g., lawyers, doctors, and teachers). The percents are calculated using employed individuals only.

ation within each grouping. The typical white-collar criminal is not a member of any elite, but at the same time, the overall profile of such offenders differs markedly from stereotypes of street criminals. This seeming paradox leads us back to some of the original concerns that motivated Sutherland's ground breaking work. In particular, focus on these convicted white-collar criminals allows us to examine a population of offenders very different from that which has been the subject of other studies of criminal careers.

When Edwin Sutherland introduced the problem of white-collar crime, he sought to broaden our understanding of the crime problem. Our approach follows this tradition. In the following chapters we examine the criminal careers of offenders convicted under white-collar crime statutes with an eye toward challenging conventional assumptions and stereotypes. In this chapter we have laid out our basic approach to the problem of white-collar crime and described the nature of our sample. The portrait of white-collar criminal careers presented in later chapters is based on our combining the detailed data collected in the original Yale white-collar crime study with information on criminal histories drawn from the FBI rap sheets. Our inquiry is also enriched by our readings of the original presentence investigations for the criterion offense. Using these sources, we now turn to a description of the dimensions of the criminal careers of white-collar offenders and how they compare to what is known about the careers of other categories of offenders.

Dimensions of Official Criminal Careers

What are the similarities between officially recorded criminal careers in a white-collar crime sample and those found in street crime samples? In what ways are they different? Are white-collar criminals likely to have the same levels of repeat criminality as street criminals? Do white-collar criminals begin and end their criminal careers much later in the life course than common crime offenders? Do they tend to specialize in specific types of crimes? Below we examine these questions not through theory or speculation but through a close examination of the criminal histories of a sample of offenders convicted of white-collar crimes.

The Prevalence of Repeat Criminals

Using the rap sheets to describe criminal histories, we find that a substantial proportion of our subjects are repeat offenders. Overall, almost half were at some time arrested for at least one offense other than the white-collar crime that led to their inclusion in the original Yale study (see Table 2.1).[1] The likelihood

---

[1] We use the entire sample in the tables that follow and a fixed follow-up period of 126 months. This means that the tables include the national sample of Securities and Antitrust offenders and the seven district sample for the other offenses studied. The inclusion of the

Table 2.1. *Additional arrests before and after the criterion offenses for all sample members*

	Percent
At least one additional arrest	48.0
At least one arrest *before*	35.8
At least one arrest *after*	31.3
Base *n*	968

of offending before the criterion offense and in the follow-up period is very similar. Thirty-six percent of the sample were arrested before the criterion offense, and thirty-one percent afterward.[2]

additional 119 SEC and Antitrust cases weights our sample, somewhat, toward higher-status white-collar criminals. As illustrated later in this section and in Chapter 3, the inclusion of these offenders allows us to contrast more directly the highest-status white-collar criminals with others in the sample. Using only the seven district sample, the rate of reoffending is slightly higher, about 51%.

We do not weight overall sample estimates according to the actual population frequencies of the offense categories. Like Wheeler et al. (1982) and Weisburd et al. (1991), we believe that the stratified sample provides a broad and heterogeneous sample of offenders convicted of white-collar crimes in the federal courts. Also, direct adjustment or weighting of frequencies would not take into account the fact that the crimes examined themselves are only a selection of offenses. As noted in Chapter 1, footnote 8, other scholars might have recommended including other crime categories. Were we to weight according to population frequencies (see footnote 6, Chapter 1), the changes in the estimates would generally be small. For example, in regard to the total number of repeat offenders, a weighted sample provides an estimate of 51% – the rate for the seven district sample.

[2] While these findings overall follow those reported in earlier studies by Weisburd, Chayet, and Waring (1990) and Weisburd et al. (1991), the prevalence of prior criminality found on the rap sheets is somewhat less than that reported in the presentence investigations that formed

Table 2.2. *Criminal history characteristics, by type of criterion offense*

Offense category	At least one additional arrest (%)	At least one arrest *before* the criterion offense (%)	At least one arrest *after* the criterion offense (%)	Base *n*
Antitrust	10.3	6.9	5.2	58
Bribery	30.2	18.9	20.7	53
Securities fraud	37.4	25.8	24.5	155
Bank embezzlement	41.7	24.5	31.9	163
Tax fraud	47.5	39.9	25.9	143
Mail fraud	62.0	50.6	39.2	158
Credit fraud	62.2	48.7	45.4	119
False claims	62.2	48.7	38.7	119

Looking at reoffending within the specific legal categories used to select the sample, we can see that the criterion offense is related to the extent of repeat criminality (see Table 2.2). At the high end of this distribution are mail fraud, credit fraud, and false

the focus of earlier studies. Using the PSIs as our data source, some forty-four percent of the offenders we studied have a prior arrest. This figure is about eight percent higher than that reported on the rap sheets. We suspect that this inconsistency in the data sources is linked to differences in the ways in which the information is gathered in the rap sheets as contrasted with the PSIs.

While a fingerprint record is ordinarily the source of an entry in the rap sheet, probation officers will often contact local police agencies and ask about an offender's criminal history. In this context, probation officers – who may get their information from local law enforcement officials, family members, neighbors, and the offenders themselves – often identify less serious criminal history information that is not likely to be reported to the FBI. Consistent with this assumption, we found that events included in the PSIs but omitted on the rap sheets were likely to be for such offenses as traffic violations, bad checks, and failure to pay child support.

claims offenders, where almost two-thirds are repeat offenders. Tax fraud offenders are found in the middle of this distribution, with forty-eight percent of the sample being repeat criminals. Toward the lower range are bribery, securities fraud, and bank embezzlement where repeat offending ranges between thirty and forty-two percent. By far the most atypical group in the sample are antitrust violators: Only ten percent of these offenders are repeat criminals according to the FBI rap sheets.

Many of the white-collar criminals in our sample have been arrested more than once. Yet, the fact that antitrust offenders show much less evidence of repeat criminality raises an important question about these findings. The antitrust offenders in the sample lie at the top of the social hierarchy of white-collar criminals described in Chapter 1. They are more likely than not to be owners or officers in their companies, and they are well above average in socioeconomic status compared to other offenders in the sample. It may be that the unexpectedly high rate of repeat offending found in the sample as a whole actually applies mainly to the lower-status criminals we study.

To address this concern, we separately examined the criminal histories of those offenders in the sample who held elite positions or owned significant assets. Thus we selected only those sample members who worked within a bourgeois profession (doctor, dentist, lawyer, judge, clergyman, or accountant), or who had positions as officers or managers,[3] or who were owners of substantial capital (more than $500,000). About 45 percent of the sample fit these restrictive criteria. Even in the case of these offenders, about forty percent had more than one arrest on their rap sheets. Clearly, there is evidence of criminal careers even within a restricted population of more elite white-collar offenders.

While the white-collar criminals we study are much more likely to be repeat criminals than has commonly been assumed (e.g., see Coleman, 1992; Edelhertz and Overcast, 1982; Wheeler, Mann, and Sarat, 1988), it is useful to consider how the prevalence of multiple arrests in this sample compares to that found in

[3] Managers in government are included in this category.

other samples of offenders. Using a sample of convicted "non-violent, financially oriented common criminals" drawn from the same districts as the Yale white-collar crime sample, Weisburd et al. (1991) found that almost ninety percent had a prior arrest reported in their presentence investigations.[4] While it is difficult to identify a sample of street crime offenders in which a similar threshold and follow-up period are used, it is clear that repeat offending is much more likely in such populations (e.g., see Maltz, 1984; Schmidt and Witte, 1988). Indeed, the prevalence of reoffending found here is substantially lower than that found in more traditional crime samples, even when arrestees (rather than convicted offenders) are examined, and when only data on prior arrests are available. While about thirty-one percent of our sample had an arrest prior to the criterion offense, this is generally true of half or more of street crime arrestees (e.g., see Tillman, 1987; Vera Institute of Justice, 1977).

White-Collar Criminals and Criminal Careers

Recognizing that many offenders convicted of white-collar crimes are repeat criminals, we are led to ask how their officially recorded criminal "careers" are similar to or different from those of common crime offenders. Our data allow us to focus upon five specific dimensions of offending employed in criminal career research (see Blumstein et al., 1986): *frequency*, or the intensity of offending; *onset* or the age at which offenders begin committing crimes; *desistance*, which examines the point at which offenders cease to be involved in criminality; *duration*, which considers the length of a criminal career; and *specialization*, or the extent to

---

[4] Weisburd et al. (1991) chose two related forms of theft – postal theft and postal forgery – that were fairly common in the federal system at the time of the study. Postal theft cases generally involve theft of government-issued checks for welfare or social-security benefits, often from mailboxes. The main distinction between postal theft and postal forgery is simply whether the offender is caught at the time of the theft or when he or she tries to cash the check by forging the endorsement of the recipient.

Table 2.3. *Number of additional arrests for repeat offenders*

Number of *additional* arrests	Percent
One	32.5
Two to four	34.4
Five to nine	20.0
Ten or more	13.1
Base *N*	465

which criminals repeat crimes of a similar type. We use the term "career" to refer to the crime patterns found in the criminal histories of offenders in the sample. However, as we will discuss later, our findings raise important questions regarding the use of the term "career," as it is conventionally understood, to understand criminality in a white-collar crime sample.[5]

Frequency of Offending

About one-third of the repeat offenders in the sample have only one additional arrest beyond the criterion white-collar crime (see Table 2.3). A similar proportion of repeat offenders have between two and four additional arrests, and twenty percent have between five and nine arrests beyond the criterion crime. While only twelve offenders were arrested twenty times or more, about thirteen percent of the repeat offenders in the sample have ten arrests or more recorded on their rap sheets.

These data show that there is a much higher frequency of recorded offending for white-collar criminals than has commonly been thought. But the official frequency of their offending, on average, is still much lower than that reported for other types of criminals. Studies of street crime offenders suggest that official

[5] See Gottfredson and Hirschi (1988) for a more general critique of the criminal career paradigm.

rates of offending vary, on average, between one and ten offenses per year (Canela-Cacho et al., 1997; Petersilia, 1980). Indeed, in the case of particularly active offenders, such as burglars, the mean frequency of offending per year is sometimes ten times the mean frequency in the entire period of follow-up for our sample.[6]

Onset of Offending

The recorded age at which sample members began committing crime also points to important differences between these criminals and samples of common crime offenders. Street crime offenders are generally arrested for the first time during their teenage years (see Birkbeck, 1997; Farrington, 1992; Petersilia, 1980; Stattin, et al., 1989; Visher and Roth, 1986; Wolfgang et al. 1987). Even taking into account the fact that we do not have access to the juvenile records of our offenders, our data suggest that they are much older at the time of their first arrest. The average age of onset for the sample overall is 35. However, the age of onset differs, greatly depending on the overall frequency of offending (see Table 2.4).

For offenders with only one officially recorded arrest, the average age at first arrest was forty-one. For those with two arrests, the officially recorded age of onset occurs, on average, in the early thirties, while for those with between three and five arrests, the average age at first arrest is about 30. Among those with between seven and ten arrests, the average age of first arrest declines to twenty-five, and for those with more than ten recorded arrests the average age of onset is just 21. These findings appear to follow a more general observation in criminal career research, which reports a negative association between frequency of offending and age of onset of criminality (e.g., see Farrington et al., 1988; Farrington, 1989).

One reason that this pattern may occur is that those who begin to commit crime at younger ages simply have more time during

[6] See, for example, studies reported by Blumstein et al. (1986) and Petersilia (1980).

Table 2.4. *Age of onset of offending, by total number of arrests*

Number of arrests	Mean age of onset in years (standard deviation)	N^a
One	40.9 (11.2)	493
Two	33.4 (10.4)	150
Three to five	29.9 (8.9)	157
Six to ten	25.3 (7.7)	89
Eleven or more	21.1 (5.2)	61

[a] Where the N of cases for the total sample is less than 968, or less than 465 for the repeat offender sample, cases with missing values have been excluded.

which they are active offenders, and this increased exposure leads to an increase in the number of recorded events on the rap sheet. Conversely, if, as some scholars have argued, people have some underlying rate at which they commit crimes or other deviant behavior over their lifetime, the operation of chance alone will lead those with higher rates to have, on average, their first arrest earlier in their lives.[7]

It is also interesting to examine the type of offense that marks the onset of recorded criminality in our sample (see Table 2.5).[8]

[7] For a thoughtful discussion of this problem see Gottfredson and Hirschi (1988).
[8] We coded detailed offense types using a classification system based on the NCIC codes, which are also used by the FBI for entering offense

Table 2.5. *Type of first arrest for repeat offenders, by total number of arrests*

Total number of arrests	White-collar crime (%)	Drug offense (%)	Violent offense (%)	Other offense (%)	Base N
Two	60.4	1.3	6.7	31.5	149
Three to five	46.5	1.9	10.1	41.5	159
Six to ten	25.8	7.5	11.8	54.8	93
Eleven or more	18.3	1.7	10.0	70.0	60
All repeat offenders	43.2	2.8	9.3	44.7	461

For over half of those with a multievent criminal record, the first offense was not a white-collar crime. Only nine percent of the offenders were first arrested for violent crimes, and only three percent were first arrested for drug crimes. As has been reported

information on rap sheets, coding up to three offense types per rap sheet event. [A complete list of codes is available in Weisburd et al. (2000)]. To create the four categories used in this analysis (white-collar crime, violent crime, drug crime, other) we further grouped these codes. In the small number of cases where there were multiple and conflicting offense types, an offense with any white-collar crime was classified as such. Where there was no white-collar crime but there was a drug offense, the event was classified as a drug offense. Where there was no white-collar crime or drug offense but there was a violent offense, the offense was classified as a violent event. All remaining offenses were placed in the other category.

White-collar crime was broadly defined and included: all types of fraud; antitrust; bribery; tax offenses; forgery; counterfeiting; theft by deception; conservation, health, and safety violations; and similar offenses. Violent offenses included homicide, all assaults, robbery, extortion, and arson. Drug offenses include manufacture, sale, and possession of any illegal drug. The other category includes property crimes, violations of probation, parole or other supervision (unless in the case of common crime offenders, many in our sample are likely to begin their official criminal careers with a relatively minor offense, such as disorderly behavior, drunk driving, or petty thefts (see Petersilia, 1980). Still, these offenders, overall, are far more likely than street criminals to have their first offense be for a white-collar crime. While this is true for forty percent of those in our sample, it is the case only rarely for those in other crime samples.[9] We do not find a relationship between the type of first arrest and frequency of offending for drug or violent crime offenses. However, there is a strong linear relationship between frequency of offending and evidence of a first arrest for a white-collar crime. For those with only two arrests, about sixty percent are reported to have a first arrest for a white-collar crime. In contrast, this was true for only one-quarter of those with between six and ten arrests, and even fewer of those with eleven or more arrests.

Desistance

The question of when and how offenders end their criminal careers is a difficult one to unravel when dealing with any type of criminal, but it is particularly complex in the study of white-collar crime. As in other criminal career studies, we cannot be certain, except in the case of death, that the final recorded event on an offender's criminal history is actually the last crime for which he or she will ever be arrested. It may be the case that individuals in

---

specifically identified as another offense type), traffic offenses, and any other categories that appeared. Some rap sheet entries were not classifiable under the NCIC codes, and new codes were created for them. Where the nature of the offenses could not be determined, they were placed in the other category. Consult Weisburd et al. (2000) for full details.

[9] While prior studies do not report figures specifically for white-collar crime, if we add the figures provided for violent and property offenses, and those for minor crimes, there is little room for the occurrence of a significant proportion of white-collar offenses (e.g., see Petersilia, 1980).

the sample were rearrested sometime after our data collection was completed. The general term for this problem is censoring.

The problem of censoring may be less serious in our sample than in many common crime samples because the end of data collection occurred more than ten years after the criterion offense. At that point, the average age of people in the sample was close to 50. Nonetheless, some of the offenders may have recidivated after this date. Because of this possibility, we raise the issue of desistance with caution, recognizing that our portrait of offenders is incomplete.[10]

While there is much debate among criminologists regarding the rate of offending in different parts of a criminal career, it is generally accepted that most offenders will "age out" of crime.[11] Seldom do street criminals continue their criminal careers beyond age 30 (Blumstein et al., 1982; Blumstein et al., 1986; Farrington, 1992; Langan and Greenfield, 1983; Polk et al., 1981; Wolfgang et al., 1987), though a small group of persistent common crime offenders continue to offend well beyond middle age.[12]

Our white-collar crime sample once again departs from common images of criminality. Age of last recorded arrest is, on average, forty-three for repeat offenders in our sample. Moreover, a substantial number of offenders are arrested much later in life. For example, forty-seven percent of the 228 repeat offenders who were at least fifty years of age at the time of censoring had an arrest occur after age fifty, and, with a longer follow-up period, this proportion would likely increase (see Table 2.6). There are also arrest histories reported on the rap sheets that last until offenders are in their late sixties or early seventies, though these

[10] In Chapters 5 and 6, we use statistical models to correct for censoring of this type in predicting recidivism after the Yale criterion offense.

[11] See Hirschi and Gottfredson (1986) and Tittle (1988) for a discussion of the nature and source of these debates. See also Farrington (1986) for a general treatment of the "aging out" phenomenon.

[12] For discussion of such older offenders, see Sapp (1989) and Shover (1983).

Table 2.6. *Of those repeat offenders reaching an age, percent with at least one arrest after that age*

Age reached	Percent with an arrest after that age	Number of sample members reaching that age
50	47.4	228
55	35.4	158
60	30.8	91
65	21.3	47
70	9.5	21

cases are very rare. Of those repeat offenders who had reached the age of seventy during our follow-up period, under ten percent had an arrest since reaching that age. Thus, as is generally the case in common crime samples, there does seem to be a decline in the likelihood of offending as the subjects age. Nonetheless, compared to common crime samples, a larger number of white-collar offenders continue offending late into the life course.

While we found a strong relationship between recorded frequency of offending and recorded age of onset, we do not find substantive differences between age at last recorded arrest and frequency of arrest (Table 2.7). The average age at last arrest for those with only two arrests is forty-one and does not differ greatly from that for those with eleven or more arrests, whose average age at last arrest is forty-five. Although offenders in our sample with a higher recorded frequency of offending are likely to start their official criminal careers much earlier in life, their final recorded arrest occurs not much later in life than those with criminal records that include many fewer events.

While our finding is intriguing, we believe that it mainly reflects the impacts of censoring. Because of censoring, the age at last recorded event cannot be assumed to measure the true age at last arrest for all offenders (were our data not censored). Moreover, unrecorded future events may be more likely to be characteristic of those with more arrests in total. It is useful in this regard to examine the length of time between the last recorded arrest and

Table 2.7. *Age at last recorded arrest and time between last arrest and censoring, for repeat offenders, by total number of arrests*

Total number of arrests	Mean age at last recorded arrest (standard deviation)	Mean years between last recorded event and censoring (standard deviation)	Mean age at censoring (standard deviation)	N
Two	41.4 (9.9)	9.2 (3.5)	50.6 (9.9)	150
Three to five	42.6 (9.8)	7.4 (4.5)	50.0 (10.5)	157
Six to ten	45.0 (10.5)	5.6 (5.0)	50.6 (10.7)	89
Eleven or more	45.0 (9.3)	3.2 (4.0)	48.2 (10.1)	61
All repeat offenders	43.0 (10.0)	7.1 (4.7)	50.1 (10.3)	457

the date at which our study stopped tracking subjects (see Table 2.7). Here there is a clear relationship; those offenders with more events were, on average, active much more recently. Accordingly, we suspect that more active offenders are more likely to be arrested after the follow-up period. If this is true, then our finding of a constant age at last arrest for different levels of frequency of offending is likely to be an artifact of censoring.

Whatever the relationship between last recorded event and frequency of recorded offending, offenders in our sample typically do age out of crime. This is consistent with criminal career studies more generally, though our offenders appear to desist from criminality much later in life than do common crime offenders. The explanation for aging out of crime in a white-collar crime sample, however, may be more complex than that for other offenders.

It is often argued that street crime offenders will cease involvement in crime as they become older because youth and agility are required to carry out many types of common crime such as run-of-the-mill robberies or burglaries (e.g., see Farrington, 1986). This reasoning makes sense for white-collar offenders only if the skills needed for offending and the opportunities available decline in middle age. Such a position seems inconsistent with the characteristics of white-collar offending, although it may apply to the other types of crimes that our subjects sometimes commit.[13] Clearly, physical agility would not explain aging out of crime in middle age, because the skills needed for white-collar crime are generally not physical. Indeed, as noted in Chapter 1, one important white-collar crime scholar, Herbert Edelhertz (1970), has distinguished white-collar from common crimes in part by their reliance on "nonphysical means" for carrying out an offense.[14]

Opportunities for white-collar criminality are, in fact, generally assumed to increase with age. As individuals advance in social and economic position, their chances to commit consequential white-collar crimes are also likely to increase (see Weisburd et al., 1991). It may be, however, that opportunities for offending increase more generally with age, but decrease after conviction for a white-collar crime (Waring et al., 1995). For example, Weisburd et al. (1991) describe a number of white-collar offenders who had lost their jobs or suffered other economic reversals as a result of having been involved in a white-collar crime. For such offenders, our findings might simply reflect the restrictions on opportunities for white-collar crime that develop as a result of processing in the criminal justice system and the social conse-

[13] See our later discussion on specialization.

[14] In Edelhertz's much-cited definition, he argues that white-collar crime may be defined as "an illegal act or a series of illegal acts committed by *nonphysical* means and by concealment or guile, to obtain money or property, to avoid the payment or loss of money or property, or to obtain business or personal advantage" (Edelhertz, 1970, p. 3).

quences of criminal prosecutions. However, this position is not consistent with another finding reported by Weisburd et al. (1991). They find that an arrest for a prior white-collar crime actually, on average, increased the seriousness of a subsequent white-collar crime.[15]

While our data do not allow us to come to a solid conclusion concerning this issue, we suspect that aging out of crime in a white-collar crime sample must be understood as part of more general life processes applicable to both offenders and nonoffenders. On the one hand, it does not seem reasonable to argue that growing stability in adulthood is a major factor in inhibiting criminality in our sample, as is suggested for those offenders who begin their criminal careers as teenagers (e.g., see Sampson and Laub, 1990). Our offenders generally begin offending in adulthood. On the other hand, as Neal Shover suggests (drawing from interviews with older, previously incarcerated property offenders), as offenders move into middle age they gain a growing awareness of time as a "diminishing, exhaustible resource" (Shover, 1983, p. 211). Goals and aspirations change for these offenders as for other people as they get older. We suspect that such changes influence the willingness of offenders to be involved in criminality, irrespective of opportunity structures and other prerequisites for offending.

---

[15] Weisburd et al. (1991) conducted a multivariate analysis of factors related to the consequences (in terms of economic damage and the number and geographic spread of victims) of white-collar crime. They found, all else being equal, that those with "prior white-collar criminal convictions, on average, commit the most consequential white-collar crimes, while those with common crime records have even lower levels of victimization than those without any criminal record" (Weisburd et al., 1991, p. 84). They argue that their results support the view that the "pariah" status of criminality does not pass to those convicted of white-collar crimes (at least in terms of opportunities for future offending). At the same time, experience in white-collar crime appears to facilitate future offending.

Table 2.8. *Mean duration of criminal history, by total number of arrests, for repeat offenders*

Total number of arrests	Mean duration of criminal history through the point of censoring (years) (standard deviation)	Base N
Two	7.9 (7.3)	151
Three to five	12.7 (8.2)	160
Six to ten	19.6 (8.9)	93
Eleven or more	23.9 (8.8)	61
All repeat offenders	14.0 (9.9)	465

Duration

Whatever the age at which offenders in the sample have their last recorded arrest, the duration of their criminal histories seems to be very long.[16] Comparing the first and last arrest recorded on the rap sheets, we find that there is a mean duration of criminal career for repeat offenders of about fourteen years (see Table 2.8). For those with only two events, the average duration of

---

[16] It is common in recidivism research to use relatively short follow-up periods – often only a year (see Maltz, 1984). Had we defined desistance in our sample as no reoffending over a year, many of our offenders would have been understood to have started and ended several separate criminal careers over the course of their lives through the date we stopped following them. At least for the purpose of studying this sample of white-collar offenders, however, treating an offender's entire criminal history as a single entity, regardless of its chronological length, seems most appropriate.

career is about eight years, while those with eleven or more events have a mean of about twenty-four years. Of course, this relationship is partly a function of the fact that it takes more time to commit more offenses. However, whatever yardstick is used, the duration of time between the first and last recorded arrest in our sample is quite long.

These data suggest two overall observations regarding the duration of criminal careers in a white-collar crime sample. The first is that the length of career in a white-collar crime sample is much longer than that characterizing most common crime samples. For example, Blumstein et al. (1982) found that criminal careers average about 3.3 years for those starting at 24 years and 5.6 years for those starting at age 18 (see also Farrington, 1992). Property crime careers averaged between 4 and 5 years. Even among active serious violent crime offenders, those who had the longest criminal careers in that study, the average duration of offending was only 10 years. Thus, while the length of time between age of onset and last arrest in our sample is very long, the number of offenses, on average, committed in this time period is generally comparatively small.

What meaning can be attached to a criminal career that includes relatively few events over a long period of time? The concept of career implies some progression and links between events. Making such links, for example, for those with only two events in a seven-year period may be difficult. Even for offenders who have three to five officially recorded arrests, the average duration of their careers is more than twelve years. Does it make sense even for these offenders to apply the concept of a criminal career?

Of course, it may be that large gaps in officially recorded criminality belie what are actually continuous periods of criminal involvement. White-collar crimes take longer periods to plan and carry out than common crimes (Weisburd et al., 1991). Moreover, it is often assumed that white-collar crimes are less likely to be discovered and prosecuted. Accordingly, the relatively low frequency of offending we observe over long periods of time may reflect the differences in the nature of white-collar and common crime commission and prosecution. This argument, however, assumes that repeat white-collar criminals specialize to some degree in white-collar crime. In the next section we challenge this common assumption.[17]

Specialization

One common image of white-collar criminal careers is that offenders specialize in white-collar crimes. However, among criminologists there is no consensus about what constitutes career specialization. At one extreme, a specialist might be defined as someone who exclusively commits one specific type of offense. The difficulty with this idea is that many offenders may end up with other types of offenses on their record just as any other person in any legitimate career might have several different kinds of jobs over time. For example, they may drive drunk or commit an occasional theft even while their main "occupation" is committing burglary. So other approaches to specialization might focus on the overall proportion of criminal events that are of the same type, or ask whether there are more white-collar crimes in a person's history than we would expect based on chance alone. For this latter approach we would, of course, need to have some reasonable basis for estimating the "chance" of an offense being a white-collar crime.[18]

Study of common criminals suggests that there is little specialization in offending patterns (see, e.g., Gottfredson and Gottfredson, 1992; Kempf, 1987). Common crime offenders are likely to commit a variety of offenses in their criminal careers, though some studies report broad areas of specialization – for example, offenders who are unlikely to become involved in violent crime offenses (e.g., see Kempf, 1986; Blumstein and Moitra, 1982; Sampson and Laub, 1995). Nonetheless, Blumstein et al. (1988) find that specialization is relatively more common for fraud,

---

[17] In subsequent chapters, we explore this question in the context of a qualitative review of the paths to crime of those in our sample.

[18] Furthermore, someone who usually commits white-collar crimes may actually be committing a range of offenses – for example, a credit fraud at one point and an embezzlement at another.

Table 2.9. *Prevalence of broad crime types, by total number of arrests, for repeat offenders*

Total number of arrests	Types of additional arrests					
	At least one white-collar arrest (%)	At least one drug arrest (%)	At least one violent arrest (%)	At least one other arrest (%)	Only white-collar arrests (%)	Base n
Two	33.8	4.6	10.6	49.7	33.8	151
Three to five	50.0	9.4	21.9	81.2	10.0	160
Six to ten	71.0	29.0	33.3	91.4	3.2	93
Eleven or more	75.4	47.5	52.5	98.4	0.0	61
All repeat offenders	52.3	16.8	24.5	75.3	15.1	465

which might lead us to expect greater specialization in our sample than in more traditional crime samples.

Examining the mix of offenses reflected on the rap sheets suggests only moderate specialization at best (see Table 2.9).[19] For example, for those who had only one additional arrest other than the criterion offense, it was more likely to be for a non-white-collar crime than for a white-collar crime. At the same time, relatively few of these offenders were likely to ever have an arrest for a violent crime offense or for a drug crime. As with other types of offenders, the most frequent category of crime is "other," consisting mainly of property and disorder offenses.

Overall, as the number of recorded arrests increases, so too does the likelihood of arrest for at least one additional white-collar crime (see Table 2.9). For example, half of those with between three and five arrests have at least one additional white-collar crime recorded on their rap sheets. This is true for three-quarters of those with eleven or more recorded arrests. While these results suggest that offenders were more likely to be arrested for repeat white-collar criminality when they had more arrests

---

[19] See footnote 8, p. 34, for a description of the offense definitions used in this analysis.

overall, it does not mean that they were exclusively involved in white-collar crimes. More than twenty percent of those with between three and five arrests had been arrested at least once for a violent crime offense, and almost ten percent of these offenders have an arrest recorded for a drug crime. Only ten percent were arrested only for white-collar crimes.

Looking at the highest-frequency offenders in the sample, three-quarters had at least one additional white-collar crime on their rap sheet (see Table 2.9). However, more than fifty percent of these offenders also have arrests for violent crime, and almost half were arrested for drug crimes. No one in this group specialized exclusively in white-collar criminality. Of course, we would expect the degree of variation in offense types to increase simply because there are more offenses.

Our discussion here relates to another dimension of criminal careers, that of seriousness. It is difficult to measure the precise seriousness of offending from arrest records.[20] However, using the broad categories defined above our data suggest an important link between frequency of offending and crime seriousness. As illustrated in Table 2.9, the offenders with the highest number of arrests were also most likely to have had arrests for the most serious crimes. In contrast, those with fewer arrests seldom had violent crimes in their criminal histories. Of course, those with many events are, by chance alone, more likely to have any particular type of offense than those with shorter criminal records.

We might assume that specialization is linked to the types of white-collar crimes that are committed by offenders. In this sense we would expect that certain skills – for example, in securities trading – would lead to greater degrees of specialization in offending. Using the criterion offense type as a baseline for such comparisons, our data support this position only in part (see Table 2.10). Securities offenders are more likely than others to be exclusively involved in white-collar crime, with about one-third arrested only for white-collar crimes. For this group, more than

[20] Arrest records do not contain the descriptive information – such as the extent of physical or financial harm – upon which the most widely used seriousness scale relies (Wolfgang et al., 1985).

Table 2.10. *Specialization in white-collar crime, by criterion offense type, for repeat offenders*

Offense type	Percent with only white-collar arrests	Mean proportion of arrests that are white-collar crimes	Base N
Antitrust	0.0	.40	7
Bribery	6.2	.35	16
False claims	6.8	.42	74
Credit fraud	10.8	.51	74
Tax fraud	11.8	.45	68
Bank embezzlement	17.6	.51	68
Mail fraud	17.2	.57	99
Securities fraud	32.2	.68	59

two-thirds of all of the offenses on the average criminal history were white-collar crimes. The proportion of exclusively white-collar crime specialists in other offense categories is much smaller, although, on average, half or more of all offenses committed by mail fraud offenders, bank embezzlers, and credit fraud offenders were white-collar crimes. Given that it is unlikely that half of all criminal offenses resulting in an arrest are white-collar crimes, it appears that some specialization is present. Nonetheless, we think that it is important to be cautious in drawing strong conclusions from these findings, because some degree of the specialization observed is likely to result from policing and prosecutorial strategies. Once convicted for a white-collar crime, we might suspect that police and prosecutors are more likely to target such offenders in the future for white-collar crime investigations.

Career Patterns

Earlier in the chapter we noted that many of the offenders in our sample began their careers by committing a relatively minor offense. This raises an intriguing question regarding white-collar criminal careers. Is it the case that offenders who begin careers

Table 2.11. *Type of last arrest for repeat offenders, by total number of arrests*

Total number of offenses	White-collar crime (%)	Drug offenses (%)	Violent offenses (%)	Other offenses (%)	Base N
Two	74.0	3.3	4.0	18.7	150
Three to five	54.7	3.1	5.0	37.1	159
Six to ten	52.7	8.8	8.8	29.7	91
Eleven or more	36.1	14.7	11.5	38.3	60
All repeat offenders	58.0	5.9	6.3	29.7	460

early start with common crime and then progress to white-collar crime? This position is supported to some degree when we examine our data. For over half of the repeat offenders in our sample, the final event in their official criminal history is for a white-collar crime, although this proportion decreases with the frequency of offending (see Table 2.11).

Nonetheless, the fact that everyone in the sample had committed at least one white-collar crime and at least half of the recorded crimes committed by repeat offenders were white-collar crimes means that we should be cautious about reading too much into these statistics. In the case of common crime samples there is little evidence of consistent escalation or moderation of criminal careers over time (see Sampson and Laub, 1992; Blumstein and Moitra, 1982; Britt, 1993). Using a variety of statistical techniques, including sequential analysis, transition matrices, and calculation of the coefficient of forward specialization, we looked for indications of common patterns in the ordering of crime types in our sample, but we found none.[21]

[21] See Waring and Bichler (1997), where these analyses are reported. Benson and Moore (1992) report similar findings based on prior offending and using PSIs for identifying arrests.

Conclusions

Contrary to common assumptions, we find that white-collar offenders often have multiple contacts with the criminal justice system. This fact led us to begin analyzing the criminal careers of those in our sample. Using arrests as an indicator of offending, white-collar criminal "careers" begin and end later, and include smaller numbers of recorded criminal events, than do those of street criminals. However, they are similar to common crime careers in that they are unlikely to evidence a high degree of specialization, and that offenders seem to age out of crime.

Our data also point to the variability of criminal careers in a white-collar crime sample. For almost half of the sample, the white-collar crime that identified them for study remains the only event reported on their rap sheets. Even for many repeat offenders, the concept of a criminal career may be problematic once we consider the length of time between first and last arrest. As the recorded frequency of offending increases, so too do the duration and seriousness of such official criminal careers. But these may, in fact, be different sides of the same coin reflecting higher levels of overall criminal and deviant involvement, changing criminal opportunities, and the operation of chance, rather than distinctive career patterns. In order to examine these questions in greater depth, we turn in Chapter 3 to the social histories of our offenders and the factors which appear to lead to their involvement in crime.

CHAPTER THREE

Crimes of Crisis and Opportunity

Studies of criminals and criminal careers often focus on those people with the longest and most serious criminal records. The study of "career criminals," in this context, has played an important part in the development of knowledge about criminal careers and social factors that correlate with crime (Blumstein et al., 1986; Kempf, 1990; Rand Corporation, 1985). Despite this concern with more active offenders, it has long been recognized that many of those who are arrested, convicted, and even imprisoned will have only one, or a very small number, of contacts with the criminal justice system (e.g., see Blumstein et al., 1986; Tillman, 1987; Schmidt and Witte, 1988). Moreover, the study of "[o]ffenders with short careers who commit very few crimes" has, in principal, been recognized as an important area of inquiry for criminal career researchers (Blumstein et al., 1986, p. 14).

We saw in Chapter 2 that those with very limited official criminal records make up an even more substantial proportion of white-collar criminals than of street crime offenders. In this chapter our focus is on these less active offenders. How are they similar to or different from more chronic criminals in our sample? Do these offenders have characteristics ordinarily associated with criminality such as social instability, short sightedness, impulsiveness, and inability to delay gratification? Or can we say that these low-frequency white-collar offenders are not very

51

different from other people in similar circumstances who do not commit crime? We begin by contrasting characteristics of social stability and deviance of low-frequency offenders with those of more chronic offenders in the sample. We then turn to a qualitative study of the presentence investigations for the criterion offense to understand how less active offenders became involved in crime.

Comparing Low-Frequency and Chronic Offenders

Social stability and achievement on the one hand and deviance on the other are often portrayed as opposite ends of a single spectrum, especially by those who view criminality as a reflection of a stable underlying characteristic of individuals such as low self-control (Gabor, 1994). Such theories predict that there would be strong relationships among stability, general deviance, and the extent of criminal activity (e.g., see Gottfredson and Hirschi, 1990; Newcomb and McGee, 1989; Sampson and Laub, 1992). At the same time, it must be recognized that what is considered either conventional or deviant for an individual is complex because it may relate to other factors such as social class, gender, cultural background, and geographic location. We use measures of social and economic stability and deviance that make sense in the context of the middle- and upper-class offenders whom we find in a national sample of American adult white-collar criminals. These measures are drawn from the presentence reports for the criterion offense.

We contrast low-frequency offenders with chronic offenders and, when possible, people in the general population. For our discussion, we define "low-frequency offenders" as those with one or two arrests in their official criminal histories. "Chronic offenders" are defined as those with a record of three or more arrests (see Tillman, 1987).[1] As we will detail in the next chapter, we think

---

[1] There is considerable debate as to what threshold to use for defining chronic offenders (e.g., see Blumstein et al., 1988; Collins, 1977; Farrington and West, 1989; Fraser and Norman, 1988; Tillman, 1987; Wolfgang et al., 1972). When referring to official data, most

there are also important differences among those we define as chronic offenders. However, our analyses suggest that those with only one or two arrests are very similar.[2]

Social Stability and Deviance

When we examine traits that reflect social stability (or achievement) and deviance, we find that low-frequency offenders are much less likely to fit stereotypes of criminality than are chronic offenders in our sample (see Table 3.1). For example, home ownership is often used as a measure of middle-class achievement, sending out, as Constance Perin (1977) notes, a message of stability and commitment to the community. Low-frequency offenders are significantly more likely to be identified as owning their own homes in the presentence investigation reports for the criterion offense than chronic offenders in the sample.[3] Indeed, low-frequency offenders are about as likely to own their own homes as the general population in the seven districts from which our main sample is drawn.[4] Fifty-four percent of the low-frequency

scholars have used between three and ten prior arrests as a cutoff point. Given the relatively low rates of offending identified in our sample, we believe that the lower threshold provides a reasonable basis for comparison.

[2] Differences between those with one or two arrests were generally small and not statistically significant. When the differences are more substantive, we note this in notes to our discussion.

[3] In interpreting statistical significance in our analyses it should be remembered that our sample is stratified (see Chapter 1). However, as noted in Chapter 1 (footnote 6) and Chapter 2 (footnote 1), weighting for stratification generally produces only small changes in the sample statistics. Inferences are made here to the broader populations of low-frequency and chronic offenders convicted of white-collar crimes.

[4] Figures for the general population reported in this chapter refer to the 1980 population of the seven districts in the main sample and are weighted to reflect the proportion of cases from each district. Data were obtained from the Federal Judicial Center, *Judicial District Data Book*, 1983, and its companion computer tape.

Table 3.1. *Measures of conventionality and deviance*

	Low-frequency offenders (%)	Chronic offenders (%)
Home owners***	54.1	30.0
Steady employment history***	58.3	31.2
Marital status***		
Married	66.7	44.6
Not married	33.3	55.4
Marital history***		
Never married	12.6	21.9
Married to first spouse	50.5	23.1
Formerly married or multiple		
marriages	36.9	55.0
Educational attainment***		
(highest degree)[a]		
No high school or college		
degree	15.9	32.7
Only high school diploma		
or GED	52.4	53.1
College degree	31.6	14.2
School adjustment problems***	1.2	7.0
School performance problems***	11.5	20.4
Any drug use reported***	6.9	19.4
Reported alcohol problem**	4.9	9.5
Base N^a	654	314

** Chi square significant at the .01 level.
*** Chi square significant at the .001 level.
[a] In some categories the actual number of cases used in the calculation of percentages is smaller. For home ownership the total number of missing cases was 82. For all other variables the number missing was less than 7.

criminals owned their own home. In contrast, this was true for only thirty percent of the chronic offenders.

Employment history is another important indicator of social stability. Steady employment over long periods is not consistent with traits of low self-control and inability to delay gratification that are often associated with criminality. And, in fact, unstable employment histories are often found to be related to higher levels of criminal involvement (e.g., see Crutchfield and Pitchford, 1997; Sims and Jones, 1997). Not surprisingly, in a sample of those convicted of white-collar crimes, we find a higher proportion of both low-frequency and chronic offenders to have been steadily employed over a long period.[5] Nonetheless, according to the presentence investigations, low-frequency offenders are significantly more likely to be have been steadily employed than are chronic criminals in the sample. About six in ten of the low-frequency offenders were reported to be steadily employed in the previous five years. This was true for only thirty-one percent of the chronic offenders.

Marriage has been identified as an important factor in reinforcing social stability and inhibiting criminality by a number of criminal career researchers (e.g., see Sampson and Laub, 1995). Two thirds of the low frequency offenders in the sample were reported to be married in the presentence investigations for the criterion offense. In contrast, more than half of the chronic offenders were unmarried. Marital stability was also higher for the low-frequency offenders, with half of all of these criminals still married to their original spouses. Three quarters of the chronic offenders were never married, formerly married, or had been married more than once.[6]

Another aspect of the social histories of offenders that is often associated with involvement in criminality is success in school (e.g., see Gottfredson and Hirschi, 1990; Jensen, 1976; West and Farrington, 1973). As in earlier comparisons, the low-frequency offenders are much more likely to evidence high educational achievement than chronic offenders. Eighty-four percent of the low-frequency offenders in the sample received a high school

---

[5] Steady employment was defined as uninterrupted employment for the previous five years. This may have involved several different employers.

[6] In this case there were larger differences between those with only one and those with two arrests. For those with two offenses, thirty-eight percent were married to their first spouse, compared to fifty-five percent of those with one offense.

diploma, and thirty-two percent of this group had earned college degrees. In contrast, only sixty-seven percent of the chronic offender sample completed high school, and only about fourteen percent had received college degrees. In this case the low-frequency offenders show greater educational achievement, and the chronic offenders are at about the same level as the general population. Among the general population, sixty-nine percent were high school graduates and nineteen percent earned a college degree.

Overall, relatively few offenders in our sample are described by probation officers as having performed poorly in school or as having had school adjustment problems. Nonetheless, there are statistically significant differences between chronic offenders and others. While about one in fourteen chronic offenders are depicted in the PSIs for the criterion offense as having adjustment problems in school, this is true for only one in a hundred offenders with only one or two arrests on their rap sheets. Similarly, more than one in five chronic offenders are identified by probation officers as having a record of poor school performance, a characteristic mentioned for only about one in ten low-frequency offenders.

Reflecting perhaps a more general pattern of deviant behavior, chronic offenders are also much more likely to be defined as substance abusers than are lower-frequency criminals in the sample. While twenty percent of chronic offenders were reported to have drug problems in the presentence investigation for the criterion offense, this was true for just seven percent of the low-frequency offenders. In the case of alcohol abuse, almost ten percent of the chronic offenders were defined as having an alcohol problem, about twice the rate for low-frequency offenders.[7]

Our findings confirm a common conclusion reached in criminal career research. Chronic offenders evidence higher rates of

---

[7] In this case there is a meaningful difference between low-frequency offenders with one and two arrests. For those with one arrest, alcohol abuse was reported in only two percent of the cases. In contrast, some nine percent of those with two events are reported to have alcohol problems.

general deviant behavior and show less economic and social stability or achievement than do low-frequency offenders (e.g., see Farrington and West, 1989; Osborn and West, 1978; Tracy et al., 1985). However, our data should not lead us simply to the conclusion that chronic offenders have more characteristics associated with criminality than others in the sample. It is also the case that the social records of low-frequency offenders suggest, in general, lives of conventionality and stability. Indeed, when comparisons were possible, we found that low-frequency offenders often evidenced traits of social achievement and stability to a greater degree than the general populations in the main districts we studied.[8]

These findings suggest that the explanation for the criminal involvement of most low-frequency offenders is not likely to be found in traditional indicators of stability and achievement on the one hand or deviance on the other. It is clear that we need to examine more closely the details of the social and personal histories of the low-frequency criminals in our sample and the situations surrounding their involvement in crime. For the remainder of this chapter we will focus on what we learned about these issues from a qualitative review of presentence investigations prepared for the criterion offense.[9]

Low-Frequency Offenders: Crimes of Crisis and Opportunity

Our readings of the presentence investigations of offenders with only one or two arrests on their rap sheets reinforce our

---

[8] An issue we will address in the next chapter is that chronic offenders in our sample often were not dramatically less likely to have such characteristics than the general population.

[9] Throughout our investigation we selected presentence investigations for more careful review. In defining the categories of offenders described below we examined more than 100 presentence investigations selected randomly from the larger offense frequency categories. We also identified particular PSIs for review based on unusual characteristics – for example, a very large number of crimes recorded on the rap sheet.

statistical observations.[10] While the social records of such low-frequency offenders are not necessarily without blemish, we detail below that most lead lives that give no indication, beyond the criminal acts for which they were prosecuted, that they would have contact with the criminal justice system. A small number of these offenders do not have criminal motives as they are conventionally understood. For example, a small group of offenders in this sample are tax protesters, who express their discontent with the government by refusing to fulfill their tax obligations. There are also some individuals who provide credible and often very sad descriptions of their unintentional involvement in criminality, or, in some cases, contend that their activities were never crimes at all.[11] Nonetheless, the accounts provided in the presentence investigation reports suggest that virtually all of the low-frequency offenders in our sample intentionally break the law. At the same time they do not, for the most part, fit common stereotypes of criminality.

We identify two broad types of offenders that appear repeatedly among this group of low-frequency criminals. The first we call "crisis responders" because their crimes seem to be situational responses to real stress or crisis in their professional or personal lives. The second group we define as "opportunity takers," since their criminality is linked strongly to some unusual or special set of opportunities that suddenly materialize for the offender.

---

[10] In this chapter and Chapter 4, our focus is on the accounts of probation officers, offenders, and others and how those accounts can help us to understand the involvement in criminality of offenders we study. We recognize at the outset and note this in our discussion that such accounts (as others in other settings) are colored by the specific interests and roles of the individuals involved.

[11] In this context, a simple explanation for their criminality might be to argue that these are people who merely "strayed" beyond the ambiguous line that often separates legitimate and illegitimate activities. In this view it would be misleading to define such people as criminals at all. Rather, we might see them as individuals who unintentionally commit crimes, either through ignorance of the law or through some naiveté or attachment to competing religious or political norms.

We want to emphasize at the outset that these distinctions serve more to identify broad categories of offenders in our sample than as precise boundaries for distinguishing one case from another.

Crisis Responders

The first group of low-frequency offenders appear to engage in criminality in response to some type of perceived crisis. Although the nature of the crisis varies considerably, in general these individuals responded by taking advantage of a position of trust that they occupied (see also Cressey, 1980; Zietz, 1981). Most members of this group had been in positions of trust for extended periods without, as far as is known, violating that trust. Examination of the presentence investigations suggests a group that largely corresponds to images of respectability and conformity rather than instability and deviance.

One construction contractor, for example, had participated in a straw bidding process that resulted in the government paying artificially high prices for repairs to repossessed homes. The probation officer noted that family and friends described the defendant as "being hard-working," a "self-made man" who was "successful in his endeavors in the field of construction." The probation officer also noted that the defendant's financial condition just before the commencement of the offense was "very bleak and very desperate." While the defendant had been married three times, his most recent marriage was still intact and had lasted for more than 20 years. Though he never earned a college degree, he had attended college for two years and had been honorably discharged from the army. The probation officer argued that the sentence should be mitigated by "the defendant's lack of a prior criminal record and by the positive elements of his past social history."

The extent to which many of those who own or manage businesses in our sample see their own criminality as an aberration in an otherwise law-abiding and conventional life is indicated in an account of one defendant convicted of mail fraud related to the false promotion of land developments:

All my business life and all my personal life, I don't believe I've ever set out or attempted to do one thing that would cheat anyone. I still believe this to this day that there is no way in my makeup that I could lead myself to believe that I was going to cheat anybody. I was forced by circumstances to make a decision as to whether or not to stay in business by obtaining funds improperly and I made the wrong decision.

Of course, such statements are self-serving in the context of a plea to a judge for mitigation of the defendant's sentence, and an alleged crisis may serve as a vehicle for the defendant to neutralize or rationalize the stigma of his conviction both for himself and others (see Sykes and Matza, 1957). Nonetheless, they have a certain credibility that is often reinforced by probation officers. The criminal acts appear anomalous within the offenders' social records, and the fact that most of these low-frequency offenders do not come to the attention of criminal justice agents (at least as indicated by arrests) in the ten years or more that follow this event reinforces their own accounts.

Although a crime may have started in a crisis (and result in a single entry on a rap sheet), some of these offenses continued for extended periods. One defendant described how once the illegal activity began it became, from his perspective, difficult to stop. "During the first few quarters here involved, I did not have money to pay the employment taxes and I kept thinking that I would make enough money to catch up on the back taxes which I never did. The withholding taxes were put back into my business to keep it running. I regret that along the way I did not go to the Internal Revenue and explain my problem." In this case the perceived crisis, according to the defendant, lasted for an extended period and involved many specific instances of criminal behavior.

While we have argued so far that offending for this group is an aberration in an otherwise conventional social record, there are some people in our sample with two offenses recorded on their rap sheets who also fit well in this category. This may appear at first glance to be contradictory. Multiple arrests suggest that the departure from conventionality is not an isolated event. However, it is important to note that the second event on an offender's criminal record is often for a minor offense,[12] or many years distant from the first event recorded. Accordingly, for many of these repeat criminals, a second arrest appears as an almost chance encounter with the criminal justice system (although it may, of course, indicate a tendency to engage in illegal behavior that is higher than for those with only one offense).

For example, an offender convicted of an antitrust offense in 1977 also had a 1974 arrest for drunk driving. That offender, who was born in the mid-1930s, was, at age 24, honorably discharged from the navy as a petty officer 3rd class and had been employed steadily from that time until the PSI report was prepared. His family owned a major manufacturing company, in which he was an officer at the time of the offense. The PSI reports that he had $580,000 in assets and few financial liabilities. There is no evidence of a subsequent arrest, nor does this defendant appear in the National Death Index files that we examined. This file reads like those of other crisis responders in our sample. The probation officer remarked that the "defendant's contention that his agreement to enter into this collusion was because of a literally life-threatening situation for his company appears credible." From his life history as a whole, it would be difficult to link the DWI arrest to any pattern of deviance, especially given the fact that drunk driving was viewed as a less serious crime at that time than it is now. This event appears as a short-term departure from conventionality. Many studies of self-reported illegal behavior indicate

[12] Some insight into this question can be gained by looking in more detail at the types of crime that comprise the second arrest event for two time offenders. Very few of those with two arrests reported on their rap sheets were arrested for serious crimes involving violence or drugs. For example, only 17 in 155 of these criminals were arrested for a violent crime, and only 7 were arrested for a drug related crime. A much larger number were arrested for other white-collar crimes, though even here this is true for only one in three of these offenders. It should be noted, as we discuss later in the chapter, that some of those with only one or two events on their rap sheets appear to have successfully hidden a more serious criminal career. We define them later as chronic offenders with low-frequency offender profiles.

that such departures are common in the general population (Felson, 1998; Gabor, 1994).

In another case an alderman who was convicted of fraud and false statements in 1975 was also arrested subsequently in 1983 on an assault charge which was subsequently dismissed. In the PSI, the defendant was described by his pastor as a frequent church attender who would go out of his way to help people. He had written a book on the history of his area of the city and was described in positive terms by the editor of the local newspaper. Describing his involvement in the crime that led to his white-collar crime conviction, the defendant explained:

> I was one of the few alderman who served on a full-time basis with no outside employment or income, and because of my desperate financial need to support my family in addition to maintaining a full-time office I succumbed to the temptation of accepting income which I failed to report on my income tax returns. . . . I have never been in trouble before and I just got over my head.

While many of those we categorize as crisis responders fit traditional middle- or upper-middle class stereotypes of white-collar conventionality, there are also many who held less prestigious social positions, although most of these were also in white-collar occupations.[13] A bank teller, for example, embezzled $1200. While she initially denied the offense, she later told investigators that financial pressures had forced her to take the money. She and her husband were unable to pay all of their bills and she was threatened with eviction. While she had an alcoholic father, her mother was described as a proud and forgiving person. Married at age 15 because of pregnancy, with four children at the time of the

---

[13] It is important to remember that the term *white collar*, as applied to occupation, refers to characteristics of a job, regardless of the pay, prestige, or educational achievement associated with it. Important in determining if a person is in a white-collar occupation is whether they are involved in the direct production of goods, whether the skills involved are manual or intellectual, and whether there is trust given to them.

offense, neither she nor her husband had graduated from high school.

Nevertheless, she had a stable marriage that had lasted since 1960, was described as performing well in school, and lived for a number of years in her present community. Her husband was described by the probation officer as a "capable self-motivated and task oriented individual." Her offense was, in the eyes of the probation officer, "apparently an isolated incident." While there are a number of indications of instability in the life of this offender, her actions were still an aberration in her social record. There was not a continual pattern of crises that would lead to criminal actions either before or after her embezzlement. Rather, a specific crisis led her to stray from what was an otherwise ordinary, though at times troubled, life.

Another defendant used her position at a bank to perpetuate a scheme in which she wrote checks which should have bounced. She would then cover them with funds from other accounts when they were returned to her in the course of her job. She was thereby able to conceal her situation, until the discovery of many incriminating items in her desk while she was on vacation necessitated a full investigation. When interviewed by the probation officer, she accepted responsibility for her actions, explaining that she always had financial problems; but when she began having problems with her daughter, she lost perspective and made herself a loan in the manner described, and then she continued to do the same thing numerous times. "I was weak and could not cope that one time, but after living with this the last year I know that I could never do anything like this again." In fact, she did not have another rap sheet entry in the twelve-year follow-up period. This woman, like many other women in our sample who violate positions of trust, attributes her behavior to family difficulties.[14]

A final group of crisis responders generally became involved in crime because of what were perceived as pressures brought by

[14] This is similar to the pattern found by Zietz (1981) in her work *Women Who Embezzle or Defraud.*

employers or colleagues. In one case, describing the involvement of a president of a national company dominant in its industry, the probation officer wrote:

> It would appear that the defendant entered into this offense at the direction of superiors. Although he knew it was wrong, he placed his job over his moral integrity. At the time, it is felt that he was not fully aware of the legal ramifications or its ultimate problems. It appears that defendant's offense would be situational in nature and the prognosis from refraining from future criminal activity is excellent.

Opportunity Takers

A second broad group of low-frequency offenders can be termed "opportunity takers." As with the crisis responders, the crimes of these offenders often appear inconsistent with their social records. However, it was not a perceived crisis that led them to participate in crime, but the desire to take advantage of some specific criminal opportunity.

One defendant, for example, was faced suddenly with a potential for the economic success that had eluded him his entire life. The defendant, a son of European immigrants, had worked for eighteen years as a transfer clerk at the U.S. Post Office when his location was closed. Although offered a transfer, he decided, instead, to begin working full time as a stock trader, a profession in which he had worked part time for the preceding two years. In his new profession he became involved in a number of violations of securities laws, although his conviction was for a tax offense involving his failure to report income he had earned in commissions from stock trading. The defendant explained:

> Business on Wall Street was in one of the biggest booms ever. People were making money hand over fist. I had never in my life seen anything like it. It was like a dream or something that I had read about in fiction novels. People around me kept telling me to jump on the so-called band wagon – how easy it was to make money quickly. "Buy new issues" they told me. "Trade in any name"; they said . . . After working so many years and putting in 16–20 hour days, six and seven days per week, and seeing how

people around me were making money so easily, I succumbed to their advice. . . . All I knew was that for the first time in my whole life I was finally making money for my family. . . .

The category of opportunity takers includes a number of offenders with two recorded arrests. One offender, for example, underreported his income for tax purposes. He initially described the incident this way: "I had a grocery store. [A large dairy company] gives rebates. I put this rebate money in my account and forgot to tell my accountant about it." However, his final version of the events was revised to admit that he had engaged in more extensive mishandling and misreporting of funds. The probation officer summed up his view of the case: "After completing the sixth grade, defendant dropped out of school. In spite of his lack of formal education, he has been industrious and acquired the middle-class comforts for himself and his family. It is most likely this ambition which eventually turned to greed that led to the instant offense." His prior offense had been a violation of the National Motor Vehicle Act in 1947 for which he received a six-month sentence.

In another case an offender had utilized a blue box to avoid paying phone bills and was convicted of mail and wire fraud. There was no evidence of any special crisis. He had read several articles about blue boxes and decided to try one. A self-employed businessman (he owned an electronics manufacturing company), he earned a B.A. on scholarship and had an intact marriage at the time of his white-collar crime. Beyond a dismissed assault charge when the defendant was sixteen, there is no other evidence of involvement with the criminal justice system.

A number of those we term opportunity takers were naturalized American citizens, many of them immigrants. For example, a Korean-born civic leader was convicted of offering a $600 bribe to an IRS agent. The defendant had a law degree and an honorary doctorate from a Bible college. The PSI notes that he had assets of $680,000 and that his sister was married to an American diplomat. He was active in civic activities and received a number of letters of support from public dignitaries. He explained his offense by noting:

This discussion of giving a small gift to the agent at Christmas for concluding the audit by that time was the origin of my mistake. . . . I have always been a law-abiding citizen and have no prior criminal record whatsoever. In the future, I will do my best to be an excellent, law-abiding citizen in my community.

Nonetheless, the probation officer noted that the defendant had been in the United States long enough to know better than to prepare fraudulent returns or to give money to a tax official. Moreover, a taped conversation indicated that the defendant and his accountant knew that their actions were not legal. Rather, according to the probation officer, tolerance of such practices were common in the Korean immigrant community at that time and thus the defendant was merely taking advantage of an opportunity that he saw as an illegal but nevertheless acceptable business practice.[15]

The idea of acceptable business practice is often used as an explanation for criminality among those whose sole offense is an antitrust violation. Many of these defendants argue that they did not understand that what they were doing was wrong, though the probation officers often raise doubts about the true degree of their naiveté. For example, one offender was involved in a conspiracy to fix prices for reinforcing steel materials. The defendant, a college graduate with a stable marriage and three children, claimed that if "any conspiracy existed, I did not know of it or participate in it. . . . I sincerely regret this and can assure the court it will not happen again." The probation officer argued on the other hand that the defendant "exercised and abused his management authority through ———'s superior market power in other areas to coordinate and police the conspiracy in this case." The defendant explained that he was taking advantage of what he thought were "ordinary business contacts."

This case involved several very large national companies which acted to coerce smaller local companies to maintain higher

---

[15] The probation officer argued that a jail sentence in that case, given the defendant's community status and reputation, would encourage Korean community members to adhere to American legal and tax standards.

prices. Managers in the smaller companies appear to fall into the category of crisis responders we described earlier. As the probation officer noted, they "felt they had to accept the market structure and practices imposed upon it [sic] by the larger and more powerful defendants." As in many other antitrust cases, the corporate entities employing the offenders, and which were the main direct beneficiaries of the offense, were found guilty or pleaded *nolo contendere* in the case.

Many of the opportunity takers were recruited into participation in the crime by others. In some cases the relationship between the co-offenders is one of equality in which the opportunity to commit the crime involves the coming together of conspirators. In other cases the co-offending comes about when an individual joins an ongoing offense either as a "customer," as in some blue box cases, or to fill a particular role, such as an insider in the organization being victimized (see Waring, 1993). Often these are very specific and time-limited violations of the law. For example, in one case a jockey was recruited into a conspiracy to fix a single horse race.

Reflecting Sutherland's original interest in white-collar crime, some cases involving large co-offending conspiracies went on for decades and participants appeared to be socialized into a criminal conspiracy. Sutherland (1940, p. 10) suggested that white-collar criminality, like criminality more generally, is "learned in direct association with those who already practice the behavior." These cases appear to follow this model closely. Offenders who lead otherwise conventional lives take advantage of a set of specific opportunities despite their understanding that the behaviors involved are criminal. The crimes are usually defined as part of the normal procedures at their families' businesses, or in their business networks. In a case that had its origins in the 1920s, one of the defendants, a company president and leader of the conspiracy, commented: "This offense arises out of family ties and relationships that predate me." The offender was very active in community organizations, and sat on the board of a local savings and loan for 25 years. In addition to the family relationships, the conspirators met regularly as part of a local professional association.

Some criminological theory focuses on the role played by the specific criminal opportunities available to an individual in a particular time and place in producing specific criminal acts (e.g., see Clarke and Cornish, 1985, Felson and Clarke, 1998).[16] Of course, all of the offenders in our sample take advantage of criminal opportunities in committing their crimes. But this model appears to fit particularly well in the case of those we have defined as opportunity takers. According to the presentence investigations, their involvement in crime develops primarily from the emergence of a specific criminal opportunity. Taking advantage of this opportunity does not appear to be consistent with other aspects of their lives or indicative of a tendency toward instability or deviance. In general they enter into a situation without a plan to engage in criminal activity; but as they become aware of the opportunity for a particular offense, they take it.

Chronic Offenders with Low-Frequency Profiles

As our descriptions above suggest, most offenders who have only one or two arrests on their rap sheets do not fit conventional stereotypes of criminality. The crimes they commit appear to be isolated events brought on by specific situational opportunities or crises. But it would be misleading to argue that all of those in our sample with one or two recorded arrests fit this image. As suggested by Elliott (1995), official records with a small number of arrests may hide a wider pattern of criminality or deviance.

One offender, for example, who made money by assisting people in filing their tax returns, was convicted of making fraudulent filings. He blamed the incident on the persons whose returns were involved. He had only a prior larceny listed on his FBI rap sheet. However, investigation by the probation officer who prepared the presentence investigation for the criterion offense revealed a number of prior incidents, including several petty larcenies, possession of narcotics, and forgery.

---

[16] We examine issues of crisis and opportunity in relationship to such theories in more detail in Chapter 7.

A similar history is suggested by the probation officer investigating an offender who worked in a bank mail room and stole $250,000 worth of securities and bonds. The offender was described as attempting "to prove [to] himself that he had the courage and intelligence to carry out the theft of securities from his employer." The PSI notes that the nineteen-year-old defendant provided inaccurate personal information, and although he was a good student and intelligent and was due to inherit $250,000 on his 21st birthday, he had been suspended from school for stealing checks and mail from other students. The probation officer concludes that the offender had a history of stealing and lying.

Another of these offenders was a registered broker who agreed to purchase shares of one stock in exchange for purchases of another stock. The defendant stated that he introduced two other co-defendants in furtherance of the conspiracy, and he taught them the fraudulent strategy of "down and out" options which were used to leverage the stock. He received half of the appreciation of stock for arranging to have stock sold, so that it wouldn't be dumped on the market and depress the price. His only known prior arrest had come some 20 years earlier and involved trespassing. However, his work history revealed that he had been employed at a number of marginal brokerage firms that went out of business and that he had not filed income tax returns for the three years prior to sentencing. Thus, this offender seems to have engaged in deviant activities involving securities over several years even though these did not result in formal arrests.

Following a pattern first identified by Cressey (1953), several low-frequency offenders appear to have become involved in crime because of gambling problems. These offenders differ from those we have described so far, in that their crimes were related to other deviant activities. In some ways this group resembles the low self-control individuals who engage in a range of risky behaviors, as described by Gottfredson and Hirschi (1990). The absence of subsequent events recorded on their rap sheets may mean only that they transferred their activities to forms of deviance not likely to result in arrest. In one case, for example, the defendant wrote:

> I have always been a hard-working good citizen, except I began to get a bit of a big head and living beyond my means along with a little bit of gambling. I began realizing what was happening, and started borrowing money to get out of debt, intending fully to repay the loans, but at the same time my earnings began dropping which led me to bankruptcy and to the trouble that I am in now. . . . I intend on repaying them.

The defendant had deliberately hidden his indebtedness on loan applications; the investigation began because he did not make his payments. The investigation revealed a pattern of similar behavior and about $13,000 of debt.

Conclusions

As we noted in Chapter 1, criminologists have traditionally searched for characteristics that distinguish criminals from non-criminals (Gabor, 1994). In this context, criminality has often been associated with instability and low self-control, whether in regard to employment (Crutchfield and Pitchford, 1997; Glueck and Glueck, 1968; West and Farrington, 1973), substance abuse (Hindelang et al., 1981; Kandel, 1978; Newcomb and McGee, 1989), or living arrangements and circumstances (Burgess, 1980; Sampson, 1987; Sampson and Laub, 1993; Sims and Jones, 1997). Moreover, those who have theorized about the causes of criminality in white-collar crime have argued that white-collar criminals are led to crime in ways similar to other offenders even if their circumstances are very different (e.g., see Sutherland, 1939; Hirschi and Gottfredson, 1987).

Most offenders in our sample with only one or two arrest events on their rap sheets do not fit common stereotypes of criminality. They lead lives that give little indication, beyond the criminal acts for which they were prosecuted, that they would have contact with the criminal justice system. These offenders do not fit easily into conventional understandings of criminality or criminal careers. For many, the notion of a career in crime belies what is most important about their involvement in the criminal justice system. Such an involvement is often an aberration on a social record that is otherwise marked by conventionality, not deviance.

These opportunity takers and crisis responders are very different from offenders who ordinarily dominate the study of criminality; however, as we will argue in our conclusions, we suspect that they can also be found among those who commit other types of crime. They pass across the boundaries of criminality because of some real-life crisis or some special criminal opportunity. Besides these instances of criminality, their lives are virtually indistinguishable from those of other people in similar social and economic circumstances.

Chronic Offenders

In Chapter 3 our focus was on those in our sample with fewer than three officially recorded arrests. As we noted earlier, however, the study of criminal careers has generally been more concerned with people who are regarded as more chronic or persistent offenders. It might be argued that only such criminals have made sufficient commitment to crime to make it possible to apply the concept of career as it is used in other areas of social life: something that has a beginning and, possibly, an ending and that involves development and identity. In this chapter we examine chronic offenders more closely. Can the concept of a criminal career be more usefully applied to such criminals in our sample? Are there also distinct types of offenders and distinct paths to crime in this category? We begin by describing the quantitative relationships between frequency of offending and measures of conventionality and deviance. We then turn to a qualitative analysis of the social and criminal careers of chronic offenders based on our readings of the presentence investigations.

Social Stability, Deviance, and Frequency of Offending

In the previous chapter we found that low-frequency offenders were much more likely than chronic criminals to evidence characteristics associated with social stability and achievement. They were, in turn, less likely to have indicators of deviance on their social records as reported in the PSIs. A similar, though somewhat more complex, relationship exists between the frequency of offending in our chronic offender sample and these measures. To simplify our discussion and display these relationships, we divide frequency of offending into three broad categories: offenders with three to five arrests, those with between six and ten arrests, and those with more than ten arrests (see Table 4.1). However, in examining whether the relationships found in our sample are statistically significant and thus consistent enough to make broader generalizations, we assess the more general relationship between the measures examined and the total number of arrests recorded.[1]

Employment history and home ownership have the strongest and most significant relationships to frequency of offending. Overall, those with fewer arrests were much more likely to be steadily employed or to be home owners. These relationships are well illustrated when we examine employment stability and home ownership in Table 4.1. While almost forty percent of those with three to five arrests were reported to be steadily employed in the previous five years in the presentence investigations for the criterion offense, this was true for only seventeen percent of offenders with more than ten arrests. Similarly, home ownership ranges from close to forty percent for those with three to five arrests to ten percent of those with eleven or more arrests. Among the chronic offenders, even the lowest-frequency group was less likely to own their own homes than the general population in the main districts from which the sample was drawn. About fifty-five percent of the population in those districts were home owners in 1980.[2]

---

[1] We did not want to make arbitrary choices in grouping the offenders in assessing statistical significance because such choices might impact strongly on the results that were gained. Because number of arrests was highly skewed, we calculate our statistics using the natural log of arrests rather than the raw scores. We refer the reader to footnote 3 in Chapter 3 regarding interpretation of statistical significance in these analyses.

[2] See footnote 4 in Chapter 3 for a description of data used to define characteristics of the general population.

Table 4.1. *Measures of social stability and deviance, by number of arrests for chronic offenders*[a]

	Three to five arrests (%)	Six to ten arrests (%)	Eleven or more arrests
Home owners***	38.0	24.4	17.3
Steady employment history***	39.4	31.2	9.8
Marital status*			
Married	48.1	44.1	36.1
Not married	51.9	55.9	63.9
Marital history*			
Never married	20.1	20.6	28.3
Married to first spouse	28.9	23.9	6.7
Formerly married or multiple marriages	50.9	55.4	65.0
Educational attainment** (Highest degree)			
No high school or college degree	25.2	40.2	41.4
Only high school diploma or GED	57.2	47.8	50.0
College degree	17.6	12.0	8.6
School adjustment problems	5.0	6.5	13.1
School performance problems	20.6	18.5	22.9
Any drug use reported***	11.9	20.4	37.7
Reported alcohol problem	8.1	8.6	14.7
N in category[b]	160	93	61

* *F* test significant at .05.
** *F* test significant at .01.
*** *F* test significant at .001.
[a] Significance is measured by correlating the trait examined with the natural log of arrests. See text footnote 1.
[b] In some categories the actual number of cases used in the calculation of percentages is smaller. For home ownership the total number of cases missing was 34. For all other variables the number missing was less than 6.

Levels of recorded offending are also associated significantly with marital status and with marital history, although the strength of these relationships is weaker. Comparing the three groupings of offenders in Table 4.1, we find that offenders with more than ten arrests are less likely to be reported to be married in the presentence investigations than are other chronic offenders. Moreover, if they had ever been married, they were more likely to have been married more than once.

Educational achievement is also significantly related to frequency of offending. Having earned either a high school diploma or a college degree is associated with lower frequency of offending. This relationship is clearest when we look at those with a college education in Table 4.1. Eighteen percent of those with three to five arrests have at least a college education, a rate similar to that of the general public.[3] Among those with more than ten arrests about half as many people have a college education, with the middle offending group falling between the other two.

Of our measures of general deviant behavior only drug use has a significant linear relationship to number of arrests. Consistent with our analyses so far, high rate offenders are more likely to have drug problems reported in the presentence investigations for the criterion offense. More than one-third of those with more than ten arrests have drug problems reported. This is true for only twelve percent of those with three to five arrests. The other deviance measures evidence weaker associations with frequency of recorded arrests. Indeed, poor school performance, poor school adjustment, and alcohol abuse are not found to have statistically significant relationships with the number of arrests recorded on the FBI rap sheets. However, we do find stronger and statistically significant differences in the case of school adjustment when we compare those with between three and ten arrests to the most chronic offenders in the sample (those with more than ten arrests recorded on their rap sheets). School adjustment problems are noted for only about five percent of those with between

---

[3] Nineteen percent of the general public in the seven main districts sampled by Wheeler, Weisburd, and Bode (1988) were college graduates.

three and ten arrests, but for thirteen percent of those arrested on more than ten occasions.[4]

Opportunity Seekers and Stereotypical Criminals

When we examine the presentence investigation reports of chronic offenders in our sample more closely we identify two main types of offenders.[5] Those fitting the first pattern are much more common among the lower-frequency chronic offenders in our sample. They generally respond to situational opportunities, but they come to these opportunities through a different route than do the opportunity takers we described earlier. Reflecting our statistical analyses, they often evidence characteristics of stability and conventionality in their social records. However, their

---

[4] The observed significance level for this comparison is .033.

[5] We want to emphasize that the patterns we identify are meant to help us understand the paths to crime of broad groups of offenders in the sample and do not provide absolute lines of demarcation for distinguishing those with different numbers of recorded arrests. In this regard, we do find lower-frequency chronic offenders who resemble in some ways the crisis responders and opportunity takers described in Chapter 3. For example, one defendant who submitted false unemployment claims argued that he was out of work at the time of the offense and needed the money badly. His employer at the time of preparation of the PSI planned to appear with the defendant at time of sentencing, and he noted to the probation officer that he was "(one) of the most dependable men he has ever had in his employment and he would definitely hate to lose him." He has three offenses on his rap sheet, which do not appear to suggest a pattern of offending (the criterion offense, a 1980 probation violation related to the criterion offense, and a 1987 arrest for simple battery). Nonetheless, like others who fit a similar profile among the chronic offenders, there are often indications of more general deviance when we look at the presentence investigations more closely. For example, the defendant dropped out of high school with low grades, and he was court martialed in the army for going AWOL. He also had a prior offense for controlled substances that was noted in the PSI (but not on the rap sheet).

crimes do not appear as aberrations in an otherwise conventional life. One can begin to discern a pattern of criminality, even in the presentence investigations. Our readings of these cases suggest that such offenders are not opportunity takers or crisis responders but are more appropriately labeled "opportunity seekers."

The second pattern fits much more easily into conventional stereotypes of criminality and criminal careers. Following our statistical analyses above, we observed this type of offender much more often among the highest-frequency criminals in our sample. These are people with social records indicating instability and low self-control. Officially recorded arrests appear to be only one part of a much larger set of deviant behaviors. We call offenders that fit this pattern, accordingly, "stereotypical criminals."

Opportunity Seekers

To describe many of the low-frequency offenders in Chapter 3, we used the term "opportunity takers" to capture the idea that some find themselves in a situation where they are confronted by a specific criminal opportunity for gain and take it. There did not appear to be a pattern to their offending in the FBI rap sheet reports, and their offenses seemed inconsistent with the more general social records reported in the PSIs. Based on the evidence provided in the presentence investigation reports and the criminal history records, we believe that this is not characteristic of most of the chronic offenders in our sample. Many members of this group – like the burglar who looks for an open window or unlighted house – seem to seek out opportunities to commit crime or, at times, to create a situation amenable to committing a specific type of offense.

People in this category generally do not fit traditional stereotypes of criminality, but nonetheless turn more than once or twice to criminal behavior. Such people often defend their behavior at the time of the criterion offense by arguing that a specific crisis or special opportunity led them to depart from otherwise conventional lives. However, there is generally something not quite believable about the defendant's story.

In one case, for example, a defendant convicted of false claims to a bank contended that he was "in a financial bind and needed money desperately." He noted that "I was about to lose my house and everything. I am sorry for what I have done, but at the time I saw no other way out." To get the loan that he needed he and his wife listed false accounts and then had their credit report changed to list the nonexistent assets.

In contrast to the defendant's representation of the situation, the probation officer argued that the "[D]efendant is not prone to criminal behavior but is miserably lacking in scruples and moral values and not above committing criminal acts to perpetuate his life style." Like many of those who fall in this category, he fulfills neither images of respectability and success on the one hand, nor those of a life which is defined by low self-control, disorganization, and deviance on the other. While the defendant dropped out of high school after performing poorly, he was honorably discharged as a corporal from the marines. After his discharge he completed two years of college as an average student. He was born out of wedlock, did not know his father, and was raised by a great-aunt. Nonetheless, the defendant had a stable marriage of nine years at the time of the criterion offense, although it should be noted that his wife played a key role in the criterion offense by making the first contact with the person who changed their credit report.

This offender held ten different jobs in just ten years, but his employer at the time the PSI report was completed, a home shopping service, considered his performance to be above average. Although his FBI rap sheet shows no arrest prior to the criterion event, the probation officer identified four prior instances of contact with the criminal justice system: speeding and running a red light; use of a fictitious name to secure a driver's license; issuance of bad checks; and illegal use of a credit card. According to the rap sheet, after the criterion arrest the offender had his probation revoked, committed a theft by taking and had a second probation violation. Nonetheless, his last officially recorded encounter with the criminal justice system occurred in 1981.[6]

---

[6] The defendant does not appear in the National Death Index, and thus we assume that he lived through the follow-up period.

In another case, a defendant who completed a B.S. in engineering from a well-known state university operated a fraudulent investment scheme from his home which realized $425,000 from sixty-two investors. Although he did not pay interest, he sent investors statements that lulled them into a false sense of security. The presentence investigation prepared at the time of the criterion offense showed that the defendant had a prior civil violation involving the issuance of securities without a permit, and the rap sheet documents three subsequent arrests for grand theft, a charge that was sometimes used for swindles, in the early 1980s.

While this record does not necessarily provide evidence of specialization in white-collar crime, here – as with many of the offenders that fall in this category – there are relatively few arrests for violent or illegal drug crimes, although alcohol was a problem for some. Such criminals may be seen as quite willing to violate the law, but they also display a substantial degree of self-control and ability to delay gratification. This offender, for example, has a college education, and he conducted his scheme using companies that he had created in the late 1960s. It may be, as his ex-wife claimed, that he has difficulty in assessing right and wrong in business matters, but his life is not generally typified by instability and deviance.

For many opportunity seekers, there are large gaps in time between arrests. For example, one offender started his official criminal history with a theft by deception against his employer twenty-two years before the criterion offense. He made restitution and was not arrested for any other criminal activity until the criterion offense, which was nominally for tax fraud but was part of a larger scheme to defraud the Federal Housing Administration through filing fraudulent mortgage applications. Several years later, his rap sheet showed an arrest for operating a gambling house. He was an average student in high school and completed three semesters of college work. At the time of the presentence investigation he was married to his third wife.

Those offenders with more than five or six arrests who fall in this category of opportunity seekers can generally be defined as career flim–flam artists. In some sense they present an intermediate category between the chronic offenders described so far, and the more stereotypical offenders we examine later in this chapter. One offender's history, for example, contains nine arrests between 1950 and 1987, including five arrests for mail fraud, and one each for "flim–flam," theft, embezzlement, and grand larceny. The probation officer notes that "the defendant is an individual who has complete disregard for any person's financial rights excepting his own." The criterion offense was a "bust out" scheme in which the company he operated obtained products on credit from wholesalers without any intention to pay for them and created fraudulent documents to maintain his credit with those companies.

While he admitted what he had done, he "verbalized personal feelings that he is doing nothing that is not done by virtually every other person in the ——— industry, and his personal feelings are that he is, if guilty of anything, guilty of 'stealing from thieves.'" One of his earlier offenses had involved what may have been a similar scheme creating a company, forcing it into involuntary bankruptcy, and, through fraudulent means, receiving $250,000 as a result. In recommending a prison sentence, the probation officer reflected on this offender's willingness to seek out opportunities for fraudulent activity when he commented that imprisonment would not rehabilitate him, but it will "remove him from the general community and prevent him from perpetrating major frauds at least during the period of custody."

In another case, a defendant had six arrests between 1960 and his death in 1983. The arrests were for false practice of law, bank fraud, two for "false pretense," false statements to a bank, and trespassing. While the defendant claimed that his wife had rehabilitated him and stopped him from drinking, the probation officer notes that he lied extensively about his educational and military achievements in his presentence interview, including claiming to hold a law degree from Harvard and attendance at Columbia University. In reality, he had just a tenth-grade education.

Reflecting this image of opportunity seekers as con men, a probation officer provides a description of another offender who had only three arrests on his rap sheet:

It appears that the defendant is an individual with tremendous potential, but little scruple. Three prior employers describe him as a smooth-talking con-man, and it appears that he has unethically pursued easy money often at the expense of his partner or employer. The instant offense seems consistent with the defendant's prior con-man tactics. . . . [He] was totally uncooperative. . . . He was not only extremely vague, but he obviously lied.

Among the lies he told the probation officer was that he was a university graduate, in support of which he produced a diploma. The university reported that he had never graduated. He also claimed to have been promoted to sergeant and second lieutenant in the army; but when confronted with records indicating that he had been a corporal, he said that he had misunderstood the question. Among his past criminal activities were defrauding the insurance company that he worked for by claiming to sell many policies that were never paid for and signing a promissory note to the company that was never repaid. Civil litigation around this incident was still going on ten years later, at the time of sentencing for the criterion offense. While describing the defendant as nervous and short-tempered, the probation officer reported that he and his wife had a stable and good relationship and that the offender was active in his church.

A similar case involved an offender first arrested for forgery at the age of 17. While still a juvenile he was also arrested for theft of mail, which often involves an attempt to obtain checks from someone's mail box. These were followed by another forgery, a grand theft of property, receiving stolen property, and finally the wire fraud which brought him into the sample. Discussing his reasons for making a sentencing recommendation for incarceration, the probation officer discussed the offender's past time on probation: "he does not report to p.o. as required, has continuously been arrested, and travels a great deal, which makes supervision difficult." Marginally employed as a musician, this offender's criterion offense involved obtaining musical instruments through fraud. According to the probation officer he had a history of involvement in defrauding musical instrument companies. A counselor described him as "hedonistic, self-centered, and overly self-indulgent, extremely immature . . . suffers from delusions of grandeur and overstates capabilities, earning power and exaggerates achievement."

While these offenders are often described by probation officers as people who are prone to criminality, their schemes suggest a significant degree of intelligence and the ability to plan and delay gratification. Their criminal records and the probation officer's report do not suggest a pattern of general deviant activity, but rather a very specific tendency toward fraudulent behavior.

Another similar offender with only three arrests – for fraud, a securities violation, and for obtaining money under false pretenses – had, in addition, a history of involvement in brokerage firms that had engaged in questionable practices. Prior to the securities offense that brought him into the sample, he had been permanently barred by the New York Stock Exchange from holding an executive position in any firm. Described as of average intelligence, he attended a military high school and a service academy from which he graduated 454th out of a class of 546. However, he enjoyed a stable marriage, was a regular churchgoer, and even taught economics at a local college.

As these accounts illustrate, even those we define as opportunity seekers with frequent contacts with the criminal justice system exhibit many characteristics of conventionality and stability. More generally, for this category, the crimes committed do not appear as isolated events sparked by some special crisis or opportunity in an offender's life. Rather we can define a pattern of offending, which suggests a willingness to seek out specific types of situational opportunities for crime.

Stereotypical Criminals

While many of the chronic offenders in our sample fit this portrait of criminality, a number have social and criminal histories that are more congruent with common stereotypes of criminality. Reflecting our statistical findings earlier in the chapter, such offenders are more likely to be found among the highest-frequency criminals in our sample. Their white-collar crime prosecutions are often only one part of a mixed bag of criminal

conduct, and their personal histories often include difficult childhoods, substance abuse, and other problems.

For example, one offender, whose criterion offense was mail
fraud, had been arrested ten times between 1966 and 1988. The
arrests ranged from white-collar-related crimes – such as fraud,
forgery, and theft of securities – to aggravated arson, a weapons
offense, and, finally, distribution of cocaine. In his brief periods
of employment he reportedly had two different hourly jobs and
was fired from them both. The defendant's mother was institu-
tionalized when he was young, and he was raised by his father and
a housekeeper whom his father eventually married. The defendant was divorced once and was separated at the time of the criterion offense and waiting to marry a woman with whom he was
living. While the defendant admitted no addictions, his family
revealed a serious drinking problem. The probation officer
remarked that the defendant was "an unsettled, poorly adjusted
young man of low normal intelligence."

Another offender, whose criterion offense was bank fraud,
claimed that his motivation was the desire to obtain money to continue his education. Nonetheless, there were ten additional
offenses listed on his rap sheet, ranging from public lewdness to
possession of controlled substances to petty larceny. At the time
of the PSI he denied any addiction to drugs. While he had initially refused to provide a urine specimen for a drug test, he eventually tested positive for methadone.

The category of stereotypical criminals also includes a number
of women. Here, too, a broad range of offenses are represented
on the rap sheets, often including prostitution. One woman, for
example, embezzled less than $100 of bank funds as part of a
larger scheme to obtain information and money from accounts
in a bank. She came from a troubled home, and she left high
school because of a pregnancy. While four of her six subsequent
arrests were for petty white-collar crimes and frauds, such as dis-
tributing counterfeit credit cards and forgery, she had two prior
arrests for prostitution and a subsequent arrest for petty theft and
providing false identification to a police officer.[7]

---

[7] We found that in the case of some of the women offenders it was more
difficult to differentiate those whom we define as opportunity seekers

Another female offender used a friend's credit card to secure eight unauthorized cash advances, along with four authorized ones. He had given her money in the past and, when he refused, she copied his credit card. A high school dropout, this offender was a heroin user who sometimes worked as a prostitute. Her record reflects involvement in burglaries, a purse snatching, sale of drugs, and receiving stolen property both before and after the criterion offense. She expressed surprise that her crime was "a major federal offense." The fact that she ended up in the federal courts charged with a white-collar crime does seem to be just a side occurrence in a long history of wide-ranging criminal activities that most of the time would keep her in state and local criminal justice systems.

These cases have a familiar ring for those who study crime, and the probation officers often use language that is ordinarily associated with common criminality when describing these offenders. For example, one offender who was arrested nine times, starting as a juvenile, between 1952 and 1986, for incidents including rape, larceny, tax evasion, burglary, and battery, is described as follows by the probation officer:

> Defendant verbalizes his desire to cooperate but never does. It is thought that little can be accomplished in this case, inasmuch as the defendant does not indicate any anxiety or motivation to change his attitude at this time. . . . Defendant seems to be an individual who is easily frustrated and discouraged. It also appears that he has very limited intellectual capacity, as well as considerable emotional problems.

Though the defendant in question was forty years old at the time of the criterion offense, this summary could easily be applied to many teenage street criminals who come before judges for sentencing in state courts.

This case also illustrates the fact that even these offenders can evidence a complex mix of characteristics associated with both

and those who fit more easily into common stereotypes of criminality. The limited nature of this offender's record might be regarded as somewhat similar to the former category of offenders, at least in the period subsequent to the criterion offense. This may reflect, in part, the limitations of common crime opportunities for women.

conventionality and deviance. While fitting the pattern of what we have termed *stereotypical criminality,* this offender also owned a small trucking business. In turn, many other offenders in this category have at least intermittently conventional lives, although the disruptions of divorce, unsteady employment, and educational failure are experienced more frequently than in the lives of other offenders in the sample.

Often the white-collar crime on these offenders' records is of a relatively inconsequential type, or theirs was a minor role in a larger scheme. One defendant, a high school dropout with twenty-six arrests between 1958 and 1987, was convicted for submitting a false claim regarding travel reimbursement for drug treatment. He contended that he had been approached by a man who offered him $10 per week to take part in the scheme. In this case, a white-collar crime appears as an anomalous event on the defendant's criminal record, which includes burglaries, petty thefts, probation violations, drug crimes, and grand larceny. This offender reportedly began using heroin in 1953. At the time of the criterion offense he was selling newspapers in exchange for room and board.

Another offender claimed, like the crisis responders described in Chapter 3, that the reason he filed a claim for nonreceipt of payment for a check he had cashed was that he "was having a problem with family support. . . . I really needed the money to pay some back bills." While it may well be that the offender did need the money to pay family support, it is clear that he often turned to crime. His criminal record reached back to 1950 when he was a juvenile charged with molestation and stealing. He then was involved in many auto thefts and burglaries over a twenty-year period leading up to the fraud that brought him into the sample. Even in the army he appears to have continued his criminal involvement. He was dishonorably discharged following a court martial for taking a government vehicle.

A number of offenders in this group appear, at first glance, to be similar to the flim–flam artists described earlier in the chapter. Like many opportunity seekers, they appear to specialize to some extent in nonviolent crimes. However, in reading the presentence investigations we were struck by the degree to which their social and criminal records suggest a wider pattern of deviance and low self-control. For example, one offender, a Hungarian immigrant, apparently made up a story about being told by the FBI to change his name to avoid the Hungarian CIA. He was known to use an alias to conceal his criminal background and poor credit history. He seems to have had an alcohol problem with several prior incidents involving public drunkenness and driving under the influence of alcohol, although the defendant denied any problem. His criminal record also includes two incidents of battery (one on a police officer), carrying a concealed weapon, possession of a controlled substance, burglary, and "unlawful use of a cheating device." Thus his social and criminal history is considerably more varied than those who fit the pattern of opportunity seekers.

Often probation officers would seek an explanation for this way of living in either the offenders' childhoods or their psychological problems. One offender, with a history of frauds, embezzlements, and false statements cases, was described as highly anxious, mentally unstable, suspicious, and vaguely delusional. At age 3 he had reportedly been bitten by a dog and the rabies shots put him into a coma for seven months. He was discharged from the marines because of "an emotionally unstable reaction." A doctor summarized his personality as "maladjusted, immature, inadequate personality; he is egocentric and extrasensitive; he is a pathological liar; has a marked inferiority complex that he masks with pompous posing; he is a psychotic personality without psychosis, acting impulsively without regard to the consequences to himself or to others." His criterion offense involved a very sophisticated fraud that netted him $565,340 in unjustified tax refunds from the federal government and allowed him to live in very high style.

Many of the offenders with longer records had some involvement with drugs and for a good number of them, as for many common crime offenders, drug involvement appears strongly linked to their criminal activities. One tax offender, for example, began abusing heroin in the early 1970s at about the same time his first arrests took place. His $60-a-day habit was supported by forging checks and pilfering from his parents. Working as a bookkeeper, he was terminated for forgery, unauthorized self-pay, and misappropriation. At a subsequent job he worked under an assumed name, and he issued falsified checks as part of a larger scheme. This resulted in the conviction immediately prior to the criterion offense. Subsequent arrests ranged from use of a stolen credit card to possession of drug paraphernalia. In these offenses he was not unlike other drug users who turn to crime to support their habits, but in his case the opportunities for crime were often white-collar in nature rather than the street crimes that are more typically associated with images of drug users.

Another drug-using offender had fifteen separate entries on his rap sheet for bad checks or false pretenses over a twenty-four-year period. His criterion offense involved working with a partner to submit loan applications to a major bank. As part of the scheme, one partner "verified" the employment status of the other partner. His self-reported involvement with drugs began after his initial use of false checks, but before most of his offenses. This offender grew up in a poor family of nine children. He was, however, an excellent student in high school who then dropped out of college after one semester. He started his career doing well, but eventually lost several jobs due to his drug addiction. He spent between $30 and $60 a day on his habit, which included abuse of marijuana, heroin, and cocaine. At the time of the presentence investigation for the criterion offense he had entered a methadone clinic, but the thirteen bad check incidents that appear on his rap sheet following the criterion offense may indicate that he was not successful at leaving that way of life behind.

Stereotypical Criminals and White-Collar Crime

As these descriptions suggest, those we define as stereotypical criminals not only have criminal histories indicating a strong commitment to law breaking, they evidence instability and low self-control in their lives more generally. In this sense, they fit a model in which criminality is just one part of a fuller portrait of the offender which reaches deep into his or her personal history and is reflective of a wide group of behaviors beyond criminality itself. For these offenders, the label of criminality appears to tell us much about who they are and how they got there.

Our qualitative analysis reinforces the statistical data we presented at the outset of the chapter. However, it raises an intriguing question regarding the presence of white-collar crimes on the rap sheets of these offenders. Overall, many of those with large numbers of arrests do not conform to traditional images of the white-collar criminal. Indeed, many do not even fit the middle-class description of white-collar crime that is presented by many recent empirical investigations (e.g., see Croall, 1989; Weisburd et al., 1991). Few are steadily employed or own their own homes. A number are reported to have had problems in school, and very few are college graduates. A number are drug users, and many seem to evidence instability and deviance throughout their lives. How then do we explain their involvement in white-collar crime in the first place? How were such offenders able to carry out white-collar offenses?

The answer to this question may be found in the wide range of opportunities for white-collar crime that now exist in our society. Many white-collar crimes do not require established occupational position or elite social status for their commission. The skills needed for many of these crimes are minimal. Lending and credit institution fraud may be committed by anyone who fills out a loan form in a bank, while tax fraud may be committed by anyone who completes (or fails to complete) an Internal Revenue Service form. Mail frauds sometimes require little more than a phone or postage stamp.

High social status and established occupational position are intricately related to white-collar crime (see Weisburd et al., 1991). Nonetheless, the opportunity to commit white-collar crime is also available to those who are much lower down the social hierarchy. One example of the availability of white-collar criminal opportunities for such offenders involves a lending and credit institution fraud in which a ninety-day loan for $2,500 was requested. The offender fraudulently declared that he had assets of over ninety thousand dollars. This crime required little more than the appearance of conventionality when the offender presented his false credentials to the bank.

Other people in our sample fraudulently obtained credit cards by misrepresenting employment. Still others opened checking accounts under false names. Some were recruited as "recipients" of fraudulently obtained government benefits in exchange for small fees. One offender submitted fraudulent tax forms while he was in prison. While this offender was a career IRS swindler, resembling our opportunity takers more than the stereotypical criminals we have been discussing, his case illustrates the fact that opportunities for white-collar crime are available to people in a broad group of circumstances not ordinarily associated with elite or even middle-class social status.

Conclusions

Our examination of chronic offenders suggests that many of those with more than two officially recorded arrests, like those with only one or two arrests, present a complex mix of traits associated with both deviance and conformity. This is especially true of the lower-frequency chronic offenders in the sample. These criminals depart from traditional stereotypes of criminality in that they evidence many characteristics associated with social stability and achievement. At the same time, unlike the opportunity takers we described in Chapter 3, their crimes generally do not appear as aberrations on otherwise unblemished social and criminal records. We describe those that fit this pattern of offending as "opportunity seekers," because they appear to be searching out criminal opportunities. Their crimes are part of a pattern of behavior often reaching into childhood and sometimes leading to a lifetime of schemes and frauds.

A second group of chronic offenders includes those whose social and criminal records reflect stereotypes of criminality more closely. These criminals are found most often among those with the very largest number of officially recorded arrests in our sample. Deviance in the lives of these offenders is not restricted to criminality, but often appears to be a central part of their childhood development and adult histories. Such offenders are well-described in common crime samples. Our data suggest that they are also found in samples of those convicted of white-collar crimes.

Prison Sanctions and Criminal Careers

Our goal so far has been to describe the nature of criminal careers for a white-collar crime sample and to link different types of offenders to different types of careers. We have not as yet examined how the criminal justice system and the sanctions it imposes influences white-collar offenders. This has been a major focus of criminal career research and a major public policy concern.

Of the many types of sanctions that are imposed by criminal courts, incarceration occupies a central place in both empirical research and in public debate. Imprisonment is ordinarily the most punitive sanction that a criminal court may impose. It is also the sanction that is associated most strongly with the criminal, as opposed to civil or administrative, justice system. In this chapter we direct attention to the impacts of imprisonment on the recorded criminal careers of those convicted of white-collar crimes, focusing on whether prison sentences influence the likelihood, timing, frequency, and type of reoffending.[1]

Specific Deterrence and White-Collar Crime

Some theories predict that imprisonment will deter sanctioned offenders from future criminal behavior (e.g., see Zimring and

---

[1] In Chapter 6 we examine the impacts of probation and fines on criminal careers in our sample.

Hawkins, 1973). Others suggest that severe punishment may "backfire" for certain types of people and actually enhance the likelihood that individuals will again be processed in the criminal justice system (e.g., see Sherman et al., 1986). In the case of street crimes, there is little empirical evidence to support an assumption of specific deterrence (Lab, 1988). At least since the 1970s, criminologists have consistently shown that those who are sentenced to prison have about the same rates of recidivism as non-incarcerated offenders (e.g., see Beck and Hoffman, 1976; Cohen et al., 1991; DeJong, 1997). Where differences are found, they often suggest a backfire effect with higher rates of recidivism reported for offenders who had been imprisoned (e.g., see Hopkins, 1976; Bartell and Winfree, 1977).

While few scholars have studied the specific deterrent value of sanctions for white-collar criminals,[2] such offenders are often thought to be particularly influenced by punishment (e.g., see Braithwaite, 1985; Braithwaite and Geis, 1982; Geis, 1982; Zimring and Hawkins, 1973). Some attribute this greater susceptibility to the fact that white-collar offenders "have more to lose" in terms of status, financial situation, and other factors than common crime offenders who are often unemployed, poorly educated, and without great personal or social resources.

For white-collar criminals the impact of a prison term may be intensified – or, in economic terms, the cost increased – because of the secondary consequences it creates that a fine or probation alone might not produce. Because imprisonment is unlikely to be a common experience in the lives of friends and family of white-collar offenders, the stigmatization associated with prison may be greater for white-collar criminals. Therefore, we might expect to find that whether or not a prison sentence is imposed influences what happens after sentencing for white-collar offending even though there is little evidence supporting such an effect for other criminals.

---

[2] There have been, however, a number of studies that focus on the corporate rather than individual offender (e.g., see Geis and Clay, 1982; Hopkins, 1980; Simpson and Koper, 1992; Stotland et al., 1980).

While the experience of punishment is often expected to reinforce for the white-collar offender the costs of criminality (e.g., see Benson and Cullen, 1988), incarceration is also likely to constrain employment opportunities for these criminals, which may in turn increase the risk of reoffending (see Waring et al., 1995). The stigma of having served a prison sentence may also serve to weaken the deterrent threat of punishment. Once occupational prestige and social status are lost, the white-collar criminal may not have much to lose through future criminality. In turn, once the consequences of illicit behavior have been minimized for the white-collar offender, recidivism may be more likely.

Prison Sentences in a White-Collar Crime Sample

Many scholars and lay people have assumed that prison sentences are unlikely for white-collar criminals. This is not the case, however, for those convicted of white-collar crimes in our sample. About half received a prison term (see Table 5.1).[3] But, as in most street crime samples, relatively few of these offenders are sentenced to very long periods of imprisonment. Of the prison sentences imposed, less than half were for more than six months, and about a third were for terms of more than a year. Only 2.5 percent of the prison sentences were for terms of more than 5 years.

It was not possible for us to measure how long these offenders actually served in prison. Before the creation of the United States Sentencing Commission in the late 1980s, neither the courts nor other federal agencies had established a precise method for tracking offenders through the criminal justice system (Criminal Justice Information Policy, 1988).[4] Nonetheless, it is estimated

[3] We use only the seven district sample (see Appendix A) for statistical analyses in this chapter. This sample allows us to control for district variation in examining the impacts of imprisonment sanctions.

[4] Despite this fact, we did try to combine a series of federal databases to identify more accurately prison terms. Yet, even after reviewing data from the FBI, the Bureau of Prisons, and the U.S. Parole Commission, we were not able to establish with accuracy the actual time served for most of the offenders in the study.

Table 5.1. *Prison sentence imposed for criterion offense*

Percent of offenders receiving a prison sentence for the criterion offense	49.6
Base N	742[a]
Length of sentence for those sentenced to prison	
6 months or less	56.8
6 months and 1 day to 1 year	9.2
1 year and 1 day to 3 years	23.6
3 years and 1 day to 5 years	7.9
More than 5 years	2.5
Base N	368

[a] Only offenders in the seven district sample are included. See footnote 3 in text.

that prisoners during the late 1970s were unlikely to serve more than one-third of their imposed sentence (see United States Sentencing Commission, 1991, Volume II). Because of the lack of significant variation in the length of prison terms imposed, and the fact that it is difficult to track the actual time served for offenders in our sample, in the analyses that follow we focus on the influence that the presence or absence of a prison sanction has on recidivism. We use the criterion offense as a baseline for examining these impacts.[5]

Time to Failure

Criminal career researchers generally define the period between the beginning of follow-up and the next criminal event recorded

---

[5] We do not examine the effects of imprisonment after other events on the rap sheets that are recorded as leading to a prison sanction, in part because the rap sheets do not provide consistent and accurate data on sentencing decisions. Moreover, the criterion offense represents a standard baseline for our analysis, since every offender has one and the sentencing for them occurred during the same three-year time period during which there were no major changes in the rules, procedures, or laws governing sentencing in the federal courts.

Table 5.2. *Time until failure*

Time since sentencing for the criterion offense	Number of failures occurring in interval	Percent of all failures occurring in interval (%)	Cumulative percent of all failures occurring in interval (%)
Six months or less	20	9.2	9.2
6 months and 1 day to 1 year	29	13.4	22.6
1 year and 1 day to 3 years	63	29.5	52.1
3 years and 1 day to 5 years	50	23.0	75.1
5 years and 1 day to 8 years	36	16.6	91.2
More than 8 years	19	8.8	100.0
Total failures	217		
Total at risk	742		

as "time to failure." When we examine only those offenders in our sample who have a recorded arrest after sentencing for the criterion offense, it is clear that time to failure is, on average, very long in our sample. In street crime samples, rearrest is generally recorded in the first year or two of follow-up (e.g., see Maltz, 1984; Visher et al., 1991). For almost half of the individuals in our sample who were arrested in the follow-up period, three years or more passed before they had another arrest event reported on their rap sheets. Only twenty-three percent of those in the sample who were arrested subsequent to the criterion offense were rearrested within the first year of follow-up (see Table 5.2).[6]

[6] Criminal career researchers typically use follow-up periods of a year or less, and even those who have recommended longer follow-up periods often suggest that two years is enough for tracking the impact of sanctions (Maltz, 1984). Using the former approach would have missed almost three-quarters of those who are rearrested in the

Of course, these data do not account for the fact that about half of our sample had an imprisonment sanction imposed for the criterion offense. As a result, our measurement of time to failure for those who served a prison sanction is likely to be over-estimated. Nonetheless, the time to failure in the sample is very long, and the average sentences imposed on these offenders are relatively short. Accordingly, even if those sentenced to prison had served their full sentences, the time spent incarcerated would account for only a very small fraction of the time period between when they were sentenced and when they had a subsequent arrest. Taking into account the fact that offenders in the federal criminal justice system ordinarily served only one-third of their imposed prison sentences (United States Sentencing Commission, 1991, Volume II), the potential impact of served sentences is likely to be even smaller. In fact, the average time to failure for offenders who were sentenced to prison is very similar to that for offenders who were not.

Comparing Recidivism of Similar Offenders

Our first challenge in assessing the impact of prison sanctions on recidivism was to arrive at a method that would allow a reasonable comparison of offenders sentenced to prison with those who did not receive a prison sanction.[7] The easiest solution would have been to simply compare recidivism in those two groups. However, offenders sentenced to prison are likely to differ from those who do not receive a prison penalty on important characteristics that might influence subsequent criminality. For example, prior analyses of our sample suggest that judges were

---

126-month follow-up period included in our study. Even the latter approach would not have identified almost half of the recidivists in the sample.

[7] We remind the reader that our analyses are based on imposition of incarcerative sentences and not whether an offender had actually served that sentence. As noted earlier, we could not identify with certainty the length or type of prison sanctions actually served for those in our sample.

more likely to impose prison sentences on offenders with prior arrests (see Weisburd et al., 1991). As a result, we might find that those sentenced to prison are more likely to recidivate simply because they are more likely to be repeat criminals in the first place. Clearly, a simple comparison of subsequent criminality for those who received a prison sanction and those who did not could be very misleading.

In order to correct for such potential biases in our analysis, we sought to create comparison groups of offenders that were similar to each other on most traits but which were different in that one group included offenders who were sentenced to prison for the criterion offense and the other not.[8] The basis we use for placing offenders in these groups was their probability of receiving a prison sanction in the first place. This probability was estimated through a logistic regression model developed by Wheeler et al. (1982) and refined by Weisburd, Chayet, and Waring (1990) for application to this sample. The model takes into account twenty-one variables including (a) legally relevant indicators such as prior record, type of conviction, statutory category of the offense, and the district of conviction and (b) obvious social dimensions such as gender, race, age, education, and social status. Going beyond prior sentencing studies, it also controlled for both "act-related" (e.g., amount of victimization, geographic spread, type and number of victims, and offense complexity) and "actor-related" (role in the offense, cooperation with prosecution, remorse over the crime, and social record) variables often mentioned by federal judges (see Wheeler, Mann, and Sarat, 1988). We estimated a reduced logistic regression model

---

[8] This method allows us to focus specifically on the question of the impact of prison sanctions on rearrest. It also assumes that the impact of sanctions may be different for different types of offenders (defined here by the likelihood of receiving a prison sanction for the criterion offense) as suggested by Farrington et al. (1986). However, while adjusting for factors that influence recidivism, we do not compare the effect of a prison sanction to other potential explanatory variables. We examine this issue in Chapter 6 using an accelerated failure time model.

including only the significant parameters for sample cases (see Appendix B).[9]

Through this procedure we were able to identify people who were fairly well matched in terms of characteristics that appeared important in determining whether a prison sentence was imposed, but some of these individuals actually received a prison sanction while some did not. These individuals could then be placed in separate prison and no-prison comparison samples. Overall, we found that the most equivalent groups for comparison could be gained by dividing our sample into three subsamples. The first includes offenders with a relatively low predicted probability of imprisonment ($p < .40$). The second includes those offenders with a relatively high predicted likelihood of receiving an imprisonment sanction ($p > .60$). The final group represents a moderate probability category ($.40 \leq p \leq .60$).

Dividing the sample up in this manner yields prison and no-prison groups with a fairly large number of cases that are relatively close in their overall mean predicted probability of imprisonment (see Table 5.3).[10] Of the three subsamples, the "moderate" category has the closest estimates, with both prison and no-prison groups showing an average probability of about fifty percent. The "low probability" category, with a difference of seven percent between the prison and no-prison groups, has the largest gap in mean probability estimates.

When we examine specific variables that might impact subsequent criminality across the prison and no-prison comparison

[9] Statistical significance was defined using a .05 criterion. The model categorized seventy-two percent of the cases correctly [an increase of thirty-three percent over the base rate (54%)] when offenders with a greater than .50 predicted probability of imprisonment were placed in the prison category.

[10] Sample size per group was important because we wanted to ensure adequate statistical power for the statistical tests we employed (see Weisburd et al., 1993; Weisburd, 1998). Using Cohen's (1988) definition of a moderate effect and a .05 significance threshold, each comparison sample provides a statistical power level above .80 – a minimum power level suggested by both Gelber and Zelen (1985) and Cohen (1988).

Table 5.3. *Mean predicted probability of imprisonment, by offender groupings and prison sentence imposed*

Grouping	Mean predicted probability of imprisonment	Number of cases
Low group		
Prison	.276	79
No prison	.202	255
Moderate group		
Prison	.499	100
No prison	.495	67
High group		
Prison	.787	189
No prison	.738	52

groups, we find strong support for this basic approach (see Table 5.4). Looking at gender, race, class, marital status, type of residence, employment history, drug and alcohol problems, class position, arrests prior to the criterion offense, district and type of conviction for the criterion offense, and death during the follow-up period, we find few substantive differences between the matched groups and find none that are statistically significant at the five percent level.[11]

While these groupings are based on models of the probability of imprisonment for the criterion offense, and take into account a variety of factors related both to the offender and the criterion

[11] It should be noted that a few comparisons do come close to the .05 significance threshold. Thus, for example, a .10 threshold would have yielded two significant relationships from the thirty-six separate tests examined. Overall, we think these results provide strong support for the research design employed, and based upon them we do not adjust for specific differences in the comparison samples as suggested by Berk (1987).

Table 5.4. *Comparison of sample characteristics, by prison sentence imposed and offender groupings*[a]

	Low		Moderate		High	
	Prison (%)	No prison (%)	Prison (%)	No prison (%)	Prison (%)	No prison (%)
Female	27.8	40.0	7.0	1.5	2.1	0.0
White	68.3	71.8	79.0	77.6	80.9	86.5
Married	53.2	51.4	50.0	62.7	61.4	61.5
Own home	52.0	41.4	40.0	40.3	43.8	35.2
Steadily employed	51.4	55.0	50.5	45.2	50.9	59.6
Alcohol problems	5.1	4.3	9.0	11.9	9.0	7.7
Drug problems	5.1	9.4	14.0	13.4	16.9	11.5
Arrests prior to criterion offense						
None	68.3	75.3	60.0	61.2	46.6	42.3
One	15.2	16.1	18.0	19.4	14.3	15.4
2–5	12.7	7.1	11.0	17.9	11.1	17.3
6 or more	3.8	1.6	11.0	1.5	28.0	25.0
Class						
Worker	60.8	67.8	59.0	47.8	36.5	32.7
Owner	11.4	8.2	6.0	10.4	13.3	3.8
Officer	13.9	15.3	18.0	23.9	28.0	28.8
Manager	3.8	3.5	6.0	10.4	9.0	13.5
Sole proprietor	10.1	5.1	11.0	7.5	13.2	21.1
Offense category						
Bank embezzlement	20.2	35.3	19.0	16.4	7.9	9.6
Tax fraud	6.3	5.5	28.0	20.9	30.2	32.7
Credit fraud	17.7	15.3	16.0	17.9	12.7	15.4
Mail fraud	15.2	12.9	14.0	23.4	24.3	19.2
Securities fraud	3.8	0.4	2.0	3.0	9.5	7.7
False claims	21.5	16.1	15.0	14.9	13.2	11.5
Bribery	10.1	9.4	6.0	3.0	2.1	3.8
Antitrust	5.1	5.0	0.0	1.5	0.0	0.0
Death during follow-up	16.5	12.2	11.9	12.0	13.5	16.9

Table 5.5. *Total number of arrests on rap sheet, by prison sentence imposed and offender groupings*

	Low		Moderate		High	
	Prison (%)	No prison (%)	Prison (%)	No prison (%)	Prison (%)	No prison (%)
One or two	69.6	76.9	65.0	70.1	53.4	50.0
Three to five	20.2	15.7	17.0	22.4	13.8	21.1
Six to ten	8.9	5.1	12.0	6.0	15.9	15.4
Eleven or more	1.3	2.3	6.0	1.5	16.9	13.5

offense itself, they are also reflective of the broad offending categories we examined in Chapters 3 and 4. The low probability category is more likely to include those we have called crisis responders and opportunity takers. More than seventy percent of the low probability group had only one arrest reported on the rap sheet (see Table 5.5), and less than seven percent had eleven or more reported arrests. In contrast, more than fifteen percent of the high probability group had eleven or more reported arrests, and only about half had one or two arrests. The high probability category, therefore, draws more offenders from among those in our sample that we have called stereotypical criminals.

Likelihood of Recidivism

For our analysis we define recidivism as a subsequent arrest, with follow-up beginning at the time of sentencing.[12] Because sentencing for the criterion offense took place over a three-year period, some offenders could have experienced as much as 36 months more time at risk than others. As in previous chapters, we

---

[12] Any events that occurred between the criterion offense and sentencing for it are not counted as recidivism because they could not have been influenced by whether or not an incarcerative sentence was imposed.

Table 5.6. *Percent of recidivists over 126 months of follow-up, by prison sentence imposed and offender grouping*

	Low		Moderate		High	
	Prison	No prison	Prison	No prison	Prison	No prison
Total failures	22	60	33	19	67	16
Total at risk	79	255	100	67	189	52
Percent who fail	27.8	23.5	33.0	28.4	35.4	30.8
χ^2 test for independence	$\chi^2 = .607, p < .436$		$\chi^2 = .403, p < .525$		$\chi^2 = .396, p < .529$	

limit the follow-up period to one hundred and twenty-six months in order to allow a standard risk period for the offenders studied. Table 5.6 reports the proportion of people rearrested in each of the prison and no-prison comparison samples, as well as the statistical significance of each of the three comparisons.

There is no evidence of a specific deterrent effect of prison in any of the matched groups in our analyses. Indeed, in each of the comparisons we examine, those receiving prison sentences are slightly more likely to recidivate than those in the no-prison sample. In the group defined by a high probability of imprisonment, the prison sample had an overall failure rate of thirty-five percent while the no-prison sample had a rate of thirty-one percent. In the low-prison group, the results are very similar, though the base rate of failure for both samples is lower. Twenty-eight percent of the prison sample recidivated in the follow-up period, as compared to twenty-four percent of the no-prison sample. In the moderate probability of imprisonment category, thirty-three percent of the prison sample failed in the follow-up period as contrasted with twenty-eight percent of the no prison sample. None of these differences, however, are statistically significant at the five percent level.[13]

[13] While statistical significance provides a method for assessing whether the differences obtained between the comparison groups are likely to be due to simple sampling fluctuations, some caution should be exercised in interpreting significance in our analyses. Our sample is strat-

These results suggest that prison does not influence the likelihood of rearrest for those convicted of white-collar crimes. In turn, the absence of a deterrent effect on recidivism, or a backfire effect, does not appear to be linked to the nature of the offenders studied. Whether we examine the high probability grouping (which includes the largest number of offenders with very high frequency criminal records) or the low probability grouping (which is most likely to include those with only one event on their rap sheets), there is little difference in the likelihood of rearrest between the prison and no-prison comparison groups.

Although these findings are clear, we want to remind the reader of a specific limitation to our method.[14] While it is possible to

ified and thus does not represent the true population of offenders convicted of the crimes we examine. Offenders are divided into like groups that represent in a broad way those with low, moderate, and high risks of imprisonment. These are the populations to which inferences are made.

[14] It is also relevant to emphasize that our analyses, as are nearly all sentencing studies, are based on nonexperimental methods. (Experimental methods would demand random allocation of subjects to prison and no prison sanctions.) For these methods, the exclusion of an important factor from consideration will lead to bias in the estimation of the impacts of sanctions on reoffending. The basis of our allocation procedure was a regression model that predicted the likelihood of imposition of a prison sanction for the criterion offense. If judges in the districts studied gave systematic and significant weight to variables that are not assessed in the model that forms the basis of this allocation procedure, we would expect systematic biases in our results. While we recognize that such biases cannot be ruled out in our study, there are good reasons for assuming that they are not consequential. In the first case, the model used includes a wide range of measures and takes into account a series of factors that judges argue influence the imprisonment decision (see Weisburd et al., 1991). Beyond this, the fact that we could find little difference between prison and no-prison samples when examining a series of relevant background and criterion offense characteristics (see Table 5.4) suggests that they do indeed provide comparable samples for examination.

commit some white-collar crimes (like mail or tax fraud) while a criminal is in custody, it is generally assumed that those in prison have a much lower risk of recidivism.[15] As a result, we would expect that the risk of rearrest for those in the prison groups in our sample would be *underestimated*. Because our data indicate that those sentenced to prison are *more likely* to recidivate, incorporation of information about time served could not show a specific deterrent effect for prison, though it could strengthen a claim that there is a backfire effect. When we created models that assumed that the offender served his or her full sentenced period of incarceration or one-third of their term, we gained essentially the same results as those described here.

Time to Failure and Prison Sentences

Examination of the timing of rearrest, as opposed to the likelihood of rearrest, can provide important information for understanding recidivism and for making public policy recommendations (e.g., see Murray and Cox, 1979). For example, criminal justice interventions that do not influence the long-term likelihood of rearrest may still postpone its occurrence. This delay may have important implications. If one can put off time to failure, there may be significant societal benefit even if the eventual likelihood of any recidivism is not altered.

[15] In addition, some offenders died during the follow-up period, and this decreased their actual time at risk. Other sample members may have recidivated after the follow-up period. In this case we assume that they do not recidivate, when in fact a longer follow-up period would have led to our defining them as recidivists. We think the former concern does not impact strongly upon our findings, because death rates are similar for the two subsamples in each pair being examined (see Table 5.4). While the issue of recidivism after follow-up has been a major concern in criminal career research, the bias here is likely to be small given the very long follow-up period that is employed. These issues are more consequential in examining "time to failure." In our time-to-failure analyses later in the chapter, we take into account these problems directly.

When we compare the time to failure for the three probability groupings our findings are somewhat inconsistent(see Table 5.7). In the case of the high probability group, it appears that, after the first six months, prison tends to slow down the rate at which offenders fail.[16] For example, only twenty-seven percent of the prison sample who fail in the follow-up period do so in less than two years compared with forty-four percent of the no prison sample. About two thirds of those in the prison group who fail do so within five years. This is true for eighty-one percent of the no prison group. On the other hand, for the low probability grouping, prison seems consistently to accelerate rather than slow down failure. Half of those in the prison sample who recidivated in the follow-up period did so within two years. Only forty-three percent of the no prison sample did so. In the moderate probability category, the rates of failure are very similar for both the prison and no-prison samples.

One problem in interpreting these data is that we have so far assumed that everyone in our sample is at risk of being rearrested during the entire follow-up period. However, the data received from the National Death Index indicate that fourteen percent of the sample died between sentencing for the criterion offense and the censoring date of the study (i.e., the last date about which data were collected).[17] Conversely, the discussion so far also assumes that those who have not been arrested in the follow-up period will never be arrested. It is possible and even likely, however, that some of these offenders will be arrested after the follow-up period.

One technique that allows us to correct for these assumptions while providing a general estimate of the differences in the

---

[16] Of course, these results may also be affected by reduced "time at risk" of offenders who were imprisoned. As discussed earlier (see p. 96) we believe that such biases are likely to be small.

[17] As discussed earlier (see footnote 15) we do not think that this biases our analysis of the likelihood of recidivism, because prison and no prison samples have about the same rates of death during the follow-up period.

Table 5.7. *Time until first failure for recidivists, by prison sentence imposed and offender group*

Time since sentencing for criterion offense	Low		Moderate		High	
	Prison	No prison	Prison	No prison	Prison	No prison
	Cumulative percent of failures		Cumulative percent of failures		Cumulative percent of failures	
Less than 1 month	9.1	1.7	0.0	0.0	4.5	6.3
1 month to 6 months	18.2	11.7	6.1	0.0	9.0	6.3
6 months and 1 day to 1 year	31.8	25.0	15.2	15.8	19.4	37.5
1 year and 1 day to 2 years	50.0	43.3	39.4	42.1	26.9	43.8
2 years and 1 day to 3 years	63.6	60.0	54.5	52.6	35.8	62.5
3 years and 1 day to 5 years	81.8	76.6	81.8	78.9	64.2	81.3
More than 5 years	100.0	100.0	100.0	100.0	100.0	100.0
Total failures	22	60	33	19	67	16
Total at risk	79	255	100	67	189	52

models of failure for the prison and no-prison samples is what has come to be called event history or time-to-failure analysis (Allison, 1984). Event history analysis treats those individuals who have not failed by the end of the follow-up period as censored. That is, it recognizes the fact that they may fail in the period subsequent to the data collection period. It also censors sample members who died before the end of the follow-up period. Because failure time models take censoring into account, we can use the entire follow-up period available for each offender rather than a standard follow-up period in our analyses. This means that the minimum potential follow-up period for an individual in our analysis is 126 months. The maximum period for any sample member is 162 months. We use failure analysis techniques to provide a more subtle comparison of the groups.[18]

There are a number of statistical distributions that may be used to estimate how reoffending occurs over time. We provide parameter estimates from three distributions that have good fit with our data (see Table 5.8).[19] The lognormal distribution is commonly employed in recidivism research (e.g., see Schmidt and Witte, 1988). It assumes that the risk of failure will first increase and then decrease over time and that everyone in the sample will eventually recidivate given a follow-up period of infinite length. The Gompertz distribution has been used less often in research on criminal careers. It allows for the possibility that some people will never recidivate, an assumption that we think is consistent with the character of our sample.[20] Like the lognormal distribution, it

---

[18] The estimates in Table 5.8 are developed using models provided in *Surfit*, software developed by Michael Maltz of the University of Illinois (Maltz, 1989).

[19] The choice of a distribution is based both on the log likelihood statistic gained and the number of parameters included in the model (see Maltz, 1984).

[20] Some recidivism studies have found that models that do not constrain all offenders to failure often provide a better fit than other models (Schmidt and Witte, 1984; Maltz and McCleary, 1977, 1978; Maltz et al., 1979; Maltz and Pollock, 1980). Unlike the incomplete models created by Maltz and McCleary (1977, 1978) the Gompertz model

Table 5.8. *Survival models, by prison sentence imposed and offender group*[a]

Offender group:	Low		Moderate		High	
Sentence:	Prison	No prison	Prison	No prison	Prison	No prison
Lognormal distribution[b]						
Log likelihood	−154.57	−449.56	−241.11	−134.23	−478.46	−130.6
Predicted percent surviving	0	0	0	0	0	0
μ	6.36	6.78	5.54	6.35	5.65	5.78
σ	3.05	2.78	2.02	2.70	2.29	2.40
Gompertz distribution[c]						
Log likelihood	−154.18	−446.57	−240.09	−133.23	−478.84	−130.6
Predicted percent surviving	68.1	73.3	58.6	68.8	50.8	59.8
θ	.01	.006	.008	.007	.006	.008
Δ	−.03	−.020	−.010	−.020	−.009	−.010
Incomplete exponential[d]						
Log likelihood	−147.16	−430.19	−229.69	−127.83	−462.60	−112.86
Predicted percent surviving	70.0	73.7	61.7	69.6	50.5	62.9
ϕ	.022	.020	.018	.021	.010	.017
Ω	.300	.263	.383	.304	.495	.371

[a] Formulae for these survival models taken from Maltz (1989).

[b] $S(t) = 1 - \phi[(\ln t - \mu)/\sigma]$, where ϕ is the standard normal cumulative distribution function.

[c] $S(t) = \exp(-\theta(e^{\Delta t} - 1)/\Delta)$.

[d] $S(t) = 1 - \Omega + \Omega_e{}^{-\phi t}$.

assumes that the risk of recidivating will first increase and then decrease. The third model uses the incomplete exponential distribution which directly estimates the proportion of the sample that will never recidivate. The incomplete exponential assumes that for those who will recidivate, the risk is constant over time. Each of the three models requires estimation of two parameters which serve to define the shape of the failure distribution.

Offenders sentenced to prison are estimated to have a slightly higher risk of failing, and to fail more quickly, than those who were not sentenced to prison. In the lognormal model μ represents the mean time until failure, and it is consistently slightly shorter for the prison groups than the no-prison groups, indicating that the prison groups also failed more quickly. In the Gompertz and incomplete exponential models, the differences in the expected percent who will never fail (when comparing the prison and no prison samples) range from four percent to twelve percent. Nonetheless, the differences in parameter estimates for each of the prison and no-prison comparisons in our analysis across the three models are not statistically significant.[21]

Overall, these findings reinforce the conclusion that there is no specific deterrent or backfire effect for imprisonment for these offenders. Whether we examined the absolute number who fail or the general distribution of failure as represented in the failure rate models, there is no evidence that imprisonment will improve the post-sanctioning behavior of offenders convicted of white-collar crimes. Conversely, there are not statistically significant results that support the position that imprisonment will have a backfire effect either in terms of likelihood or timing of

---

does not assume that some individuals have a zero probability of recidivism. Rather, the probability that some will survive infinitely is an outcome of the values of the parameters of the distribution, specifically negative estimates for Δ (Cox and Oakes, 1984, p. 30).

[21] Using Surfit we developed contours for each of the six distributions based on a ninety-five percent confidence interval. In each of the pairs of prison and no-prison samples the contours were found to overlap. We want to thank Michael Maltz for his assistance in constructing and interpreting these analyses.

recidivism. There also appears to be little difference in the effectiveness of sanctions across broad groups of offenders. There were no statistically significant impacts of imprisonment in any of the matched samples.

Frequency and Type of Offending

Although prison appears to have little impact on the likelihood of or time to failure, it might be that there is an effect on the frequency of offending following the criterion offense. Table 5.9 presents the relationship between imprisonment and number of subsequent arrests for each of the three offender groupings. The distributions in the low and high probability groups are very similar.[22] Between fifty and sixty-two percent of the offenders in both samples have one or two subsequent arrests, and between eighty and ninety percent of the offenders who recidivated in the high and low groups had five or fewer subsequent rap sheet entries. The correlation coefficient measuring the relationship between an imprisonment sentence and number of subsequent arrests for each of the comparisons confirms these observations. The relationships are small and not statistically significant.

While there are larger differences in number of subsequent arrests for the moderate probability group, the effect is again in the direction of backfire rather than deterrence. Offenders sentenced to a prison term, on average, committed a larger number of offenses in the follow-up period than those not sentenced to prison. However, in part because of the relatively small number of repeat offenders included in these comparisons, such differences are not statistically significant, and thus not reliable enough to generalize beyond this specific sample.

To examine the type of crime committed subsequent to the criterion offense, we classified offenses as white-collar, drug-related,

---

[22] This is implied by simple extrapolation of the hazard rates from the preceding analyses. The appropriateness of this simple extension, however, is unknown and therefore we take the approach described here.

Table 5.9. *Number of arrests after sentencing for the criterion offense for those who reoffend, by prison sentence imposed and offender groupings*

	Offender groups and prison sentence imposed					
	Low		Moderate		High	
	Prison	No prison	Prison	No prison	Prison	No prison
Number of arrests	Cumulative percentage		Cumulative percentage		Cumulative percentage	
One	45.5	41.7	42.4	57.9	37.3	37.5
Two	59.1	61.7	60.6	73.7	58.2	50.0
Three to five	81.8	88.3	87.9	94.7	89.6	81.3
Six or more	100.0	100.0	100.0	100.0	100.0	100.0
Total N	22	60	33	19	67	16
Correlation coefficient	$.007 \ p = .947$		$.189 \ p = .179$		$-.104 \ p = .349$	

Table 5.10. *Type of crime for first post-sentencing arrest for those who reoffend, by prison sentence imposed and offender groupings*

	Low		Moderate		High	
	Prison (%)	No prison (%)	Prison (%)	No prison (%)	Prison (%)	No prison (%)
White-collar offense	20.0	35.6	27.3	31.6	31.7	40.0
Drug offense	15.0	6.8	9.1	5.3	11.1	6.7
Violent offense	5.0	11.9	9.1	5.3	15.9	6.7
Other offense	60.0	45.8	54.5	57.9	41.3	46.7
Base *n*	20	59	33	19	63	15

violent, or other (see Table 5.10).[23] Again, because the number of cases in each crime category is small, it would be wrong to draw strong conclusions. Nonetheless, these data also suggest that the influence of imprisonment on future arrests is not very great. For each of the six subsamples, the "other" crime category, which includes property crimes, family disputes, public disturbance or nuisance offense, gambling, and immigration offenses, is the largest, followed by white-collar offenses.

Conclusions

It has often been assumed by scholars and policy makers that white-collar criminals will be particularly affected by prison sanctions. Our analyses suggest that this assumption is wrong, at least as regards official reoffending among those convicted of white-

---

[23] See footnote 8 in Chapter 2 for a description of this typology.

collar crimes in the federal courts. A prison sentence does not have a specific deterrent effect on rearrest whether we examine the likelihood, timing, frequency, or type of recidivism. These data also do not support the opposite argument that suggests that imprisonment sanctions will backfire and lead to more serious future offending.

While these findings are intriguing, they suggest the importance of looking more generally at factors that influence recidivism in a white-collar crime sample. We turn to this question in Chapter 6, where we will explore the relative influence of other sanctions such as fines or probation, as well as relevant social and demographic measures.

Understanding Recidivism

In the previous chapters our aim was to provide a detailed portrait of the criminal careers of offenders convicted of white-collar crimes. Aside from noting the general characteristics that were related to different types of offending patterns and identifying the specific impacts of prison sentences on rearrest after the criterion offense, we focused more on description than on explanation. In this chapter our aim is different. We want to step back from these descriptions to see if knowledge of an offender's social and criminal background can help us to explain his or her future involvement in crime as evidenced in the FBI rap sheets. We begin the chapter by identifying variables that prior research and theory would suggest are important for modeling recidivism in a white-collar crime sample. We then examine the impacts of these measures on rearrest in the context of a multivariate accelerated failure time model.

Modeling Recidivism

Prior studies of recidivism suggest a number of different factors that influence reoffending. For example, as noted in earlier chapters, social stability and achievement on the one hand and deviance on the other have often been linked to criminality (e.g., see Gottfredson and Hirschi, 1990). Others have emphasized the importance of prior criminal behavior (e.g., see Farrington et al., 1988; Wolfgang et al., 1987). In the case of white collar crime, criminologists have been particularly concerned with the impacts of both formal and informal sanctions on future offending (e.g., see Benson and Moore, 1992). In this section we describe the specific measures that we use to model recidivism in our sample.

Social Stability and Deviance

A number of scholars suggest that an individual's bonds to community, peers, and family will impact upon his or her involvement in crime (e.g., see Ageton, 1983; Elliott et al., 1985; Rodriguez and Weisburd, 1991; Sampson and Laub, 1995). In this context, social stability – as reflected by economic or educational achievement or by family or community ties – is generally assumed to inhibit criminality.

Marriage, in particular, has been identified as decreasing the likelihood of reoffending (Farrington, 1995; Sampson and Laub, 1995; Warr, 1998). In Chapters 3 and 4 we saw that marital status was related to frequency of offending. Here we examine the impact of marital status – measured by contrasting those people who were married, formerly married, or never married at the time of sentencing for the criterion offense (see Table 6.1) – on rearrest after sentencing for the criterion offense.[1]

Three other measures that reflect stable community and family ties are also included in our analysis: home ownership, parenthood, and positive community reputation. We have already described the importance of home ownership as an indicator of

---

[1] We recognize that the relationship between marriage and criminality may be complex, and such complexity may be missed in the measurement we use here. For example, Warr (1998) suggests that the impact of marriage on criminal careers may be the result of changing peer networks. Our data do not allow us to examine the impacts of marital status on peer networks for the offenders we study. Nonetheless, we believe that marital status at the time of the offense does provide an important indicator of stable family ties as reflected by its significance in the model we estimate later in the chapter.

Table 6.1. *Description of variables used in the multivariate analysis of time to failure*

Variable	Measure
I. Social stability and deviance	
Marital status	Three-category nominal variable:
	Married at time of offense
	Formerly married
	Never married (excluded category)
Home ownership	Binary, 1 = own home, 0 = not
Parenthood	Number of children
Community reputation	Binary, 1 = positive, 0 = other
Class position	Five-category nominal variable:
	Owner
	Officer
	Manager
	Sole proprieter
	Worker (excluded category)
Years of formal education	Number of years of education
Alcohol abuse	Binary, 1 = yes, 0 = no
Drug use	Binary, 1 = yes, 0 = no
Poor school performance	Binary, 1 = yes, 0 = no
II. Dimensions of prior criminality	
Number of prior arrests	Number of prior arrests
Age of onset of offending	Age at first arrest on rap sheet
Most serious prior arrest	Six-level ordinal scale ranging from "no prior convictions" to "highest felony offenses"
III. Formal and informal sanctions	
Prison sentence imposed	Binary, 1 = yes, 0 = no
Probation sentence imposed	Number of months probation
Fine	Binary, 1 = yes, 0 = no
Loss of job	Binary, 1 = yes, 0 = no
Bankruptcy	Binary, 1 = yes, 0 = no
Family suffering	Binary, 1 = yes, 0 = no
Remorse	Binary, 1 = yes, 0 = no

Table 6.1. *(cont.)*

Variable	Measure
IV. Other variables	
Gender	Binary, 1 = female, 0 = male
Age	Years of age
Race	Binary 1 = white, 0 = nonwhite
Statutory category of offense	Eight-category nominal variable:
	Antitrust
	Bank
	Bribery
	Credit fraud
	False claims
	Mail fraud
	Securities
	Tax (excluded category)

middle-class achievement and stability in American society (see Perin, 1977). Parenthood has also been described in criminal career research as a factor in increasing conventional community ties and social responsibility (see Labouvie, 1996; Schmidt and Witte, 1988).

"Positive community reputation" is not ordinarily part of criminal career studies, in good part because common crime offenders are generally not thought to be well-regarded in the communities in which they live. We coded positive community reputation as present when the probation officer who prepared the presentence investigation stated that the offender had a favorable reputation in the community. Although subjective and possibly prone to manipulation by an experienced defense lawyer, it identifies in a broad way those in the sample who were perceived by the probation officers to have strong conventional bonds to the community. It was ordinarily noted when a defendant "had an unusual degree of influence or stature in the community" (Weisburd et al., 1991, p. 68). About fifteen percent of those in the sample were identified by probation officers as having a favorable community reputation.

Education and work have long been used as indicators of social stability and achievement in American society. Staying in school longer and holding jobs of responsibility and authority are generally considered to be inconsistent with impulsivity and inability to delay gratification, characteristics that are often associated with criminality (see Deng and Zang, 1998; Hirschi and Gottfredson, 1987; Mak, 1991). While such measures are thought to impact upon criminality, in many recidivism studies they are ignored because street crime samples are generally dominated by people with little educational achievement and with low class position. In this sample, however, there is considerable variation in terms of both social class and educational achievement, and measures of both are included in our multivariate analysis of time to failure. In measuring social class we distinguish between owners, officers, managers, sole proprietors, and workers.[2] Educational achievement is measured by number of years of formal education.

Just as social stability and achievement are thought by many criminologists to inhibit criminality, more general deviant behavior – even if it is noncriminal or never leads to an arrest – is assumed to increase the risk of reoffending (Schmidt and Witte, 1988). Gottfredson and Hirschi (1990) argue that an individual's levels of involvement in all forms of deviant and criminal behavior are simply indicators of a single underlying characteristic of low self-control. We measure these related forms of deviance using three measures introduced in Chapter 3: evidence of alcohol problems, involvement with illicit drugs, and indications of poor performance in school. We examine later in the chapter whether higher rates of more general deviance influence rearrest in a white-collar crime sample.

While the Wheeler, Weisburd, and Bode (1988) data are rich in detail as compared with data collected in other studies based on official information, they are necessarily deficient in defining

---

[2] The distribution of social class, as would be expected in a sample of white-collar offenders, is weighted toward higher class position. About one-third of the sample are owners or officers.

specific measure of social stability, social ties, and deviance. For example, we do not directly assess involvement with "delinquent peers," a variable that self-report studies have identified as central to understanding criminal involvement among youth (e.g., see Ageton, 1983; Elliott et al., 1985; Rodriguez and Weisburd, 1991). Nor do we have information on the offender's general attitudes toward deviance, another measure that has been found in self-report studies to be predictive of criminal involvement. We have already speculated on the importance of such factors in explaining involvement in crime in our qualitative analyses of the presentence investigations in Chapters 3 and 4, and we will again raise them in our discussion in Chapter 7. However, we remind the reader here that the quantitative models we estimate later in the chapter do not take them into account.

Dimensions of Criminal Careers

Research on criminal careers suggests that several dimensions of prior criminality are important for predicting future offending (see Farrington et al., 1988; Langan and Farrington, 1983; Petersilia, 1980; Tracy and Kempf-Leonard, 1996). We examine three variables that describe prior criminality: the number of arrests prior to the criterion offense, the age of onset of offending (as indicated by age at the date of the first arrest), and the level of seriousness of the most serious prior arrest recorded.[3] It is generally assumed that the earlier the onset of criminality, the more frequent the involvement in crime, and the more aggravated the seriousness of prior offenses, the more likely is the offender to recidivate.

Formal and Informal Sanctions

The impact of criminal sanctions on reoffending is an important research and policy concern. While the results presented in

[3] This seriousness measure was used both by Wheeler, Weisburd, Waring, and Bode (1988) and by Weisburd et al. (1991). It uses data on prior arrests that are drawn from the presentence investigations, and it is based on the New York State Penal Code in the late 1980s.

Chapter 5 show that a prison sentence in itself does not influence rearrest subsequent to sentencing for the criterion offense, the possible influence of probation sentences and fines have not yet been examined.

Prior criminal career studies suggest that there may be a backfire rather than a deterrent effect of probation on recidivism (Farrington et al., 1986; Petersilia and Turner, 1986). This is generally explained in reference to the increased surveillance that accompanies probation supervision. Such surveillance, irrespective of actual offending patterns, makes it likelier that criminal behavior will be identified and recorded by criminal justice agents.

There has been comparatively little analysis to date on the relationship between fines and recidivism, and existing studies often provide contradictory results (Gordon and Glaser, 1991). Nonetheless, some scholars have argued that it is particularly important to take fines into account when studying white-collar criminals (Coffee, 1980; Kennedy, 1985). Such penalties are likely to be used more often in white-collar crime sentencing than in street crime sentencing (see Weisburd et al., 1991). Moreover, fines may be a more consequential formal sanction for offenders who, like many of those in our sample, have assets to lose as a result of legal sanctions.

Judges commonly imposed both fines and probation as sanctions for the criterion offense.[4] In almost one-third of the cases, fines were imposed, and about eight in ten offenders in the sample received some type of probation sanction. We assess the influence of formal sanctions on rearrest with three separate measures: whether a prison sentence had been imposed;[5] the number

---

[4] In some cases, offenders were ordered to make restitution or perform community service or sentenced to other nonstandard sanctions, but these were too uncommon and varied so widely in their specific dimensions that it was not possible to model them [See Weisburd et al. (1991) for a complete discussion of other sentences imposed].

[5] While we have already reviewed the impact of a prison sentence on rearrest in Chapter 5, we include this measure in our multivariate analysis in order to ensure that the effects of prison sanctions are not biasing other estimates in our model.

of months of probation to which the offender was sentenced; and whether a fine was imposed.

While prior studies of recidivism have not focused on informal sanctions that result from criminal processing, movement through the legal process is often assumed to exact a greater toll on white-collar offenders than other criminals. Indeed, a number of scholars suggest that the effects of prosecution and conviction on the lives of white-collar defendants may be a greater punishment than the actual legal penalties that they face (e.g., see Benson, 1982). Therefore, our analysis includes three measures of informal sanctions: whether an individual lost his or her job as a result of prosecution for the criterion crime; whether there was a business or personal bankruptcy that was attributed to the offense or its prosecution; and whether there was any mention of family suffering as a result of the offense or its prosecution.[6] We also examine a related measure of the defendant's response to prosecution: whether the defendant expressed remorse for the offense.

Other Variables: Gender, Race, Age, and Statutory Offense

Demographic characteristics impact upon many social phenomena and have also been found to be important in understanding recidivism. For example, it has generally been reported that women are less likely to recidivate than men (e.g., see Schulke, 1993), and that whites are less likely to recidivate than nonwhites (Schmidt and Witte, 1988). As discussed in Chapter 3, it is generally assumed that criminals will "age out" of crime, and a number of studies of recidivism have supported the hypothesis that the risk of reoffending decreases with the age of the offender (Wilson and Hernstein, 1985). Accordingly, in explaining recidivism we include measures of gender, race, and age.

Finally, we take into account in our analysis a set of dummy variables indicating the statutory category of the criterion offense. There are important differences between both the nature of the

---

[6] The source of the report of family suffering could be the probation officer, family members, or the offender.

offenses and the types of offenders convicted under distinct crime statutes (see Weisburd et al., 1991). Accordingly, there may be something about either the nature of the offenses themselves or the social responses to them that either increases or decreases the risk of rearrest even after other variables have been controlled for.

Explaining Recidivism

We use a multivariate accelerated failure time analysis to measure the impacts of these variables on rearrest after the criterion offense. As discussed in Chapter 5, failure time models allow us to take into account problems of censoring: in our case the fact that some people in the sample died before the end of the follow-up period and others may be rearrested for the first time after the follow-up period. Just as in simpler regression approaches, the estimated coefficients tell what effect a specific variable has when all other variables in the model are held constant. Table 6.2 presents the parameter estimates for each of the variables in the model based on an accelerated failure-time analysis of rearrest using a lognormal distribution.[7] The dependent variable in the

---

[7] The model was estimated using the SAS Lifereg procedure (SAS Institute, 1990). The first step in the estimation of an accelerated failure time analysis is the identification of the distribution that best describes the error term and, thus, describes the shape of the distribution over time. For this analysis, it was determined, based on the comparison of log likelihoods for a number of possible distributions, that the best specification of the time effect is the lognormal distribution. In a lognormal distribution, the monthly risk of recidivism increases with time in the early time periods, peaks, and then decreases with time. The lognormal distribution is one that has frequently been found to fit recidivism data well. Schmidt and Witte (1988), for example, found that it fit their data on the time until return to custody for released North Carolina prisoners. The effects of covariates did not differ substantially between specifications. Other distributions tested include log-logistic, Weibull, and Gamma distributions. There is no reason to suspect that the overall conclusions would be very different between the lognormal and incomplete failure solutions such as those presented in Chapter 3.

Table 6.2. *Accelerated failure time model of recidivism (lognormal model)*

Variable	Estimate
Constant	4.91***
Normal scale	2.05
I. Social stability and deviance	
Marital status[a]	—*
Formerly married	0.02
Married	0.71*
(single)	
Home owner	0.14
Number of children	−0.03
Positive reputation in community	0.39
Class[a]	
Owner	−0.53
Officer	0.70
Manager	−0.17
Sole proprietor	−0.68
(worker)	
Years of education	0.07
Alcohol abuse	−0.56
Any drug use	−0.64*
Poor school performance	−0.10
II. Dimensions of prior criminality	
Number of prior arrests	−0.10*
Age at first arrest	0.00
Most serious prior arrest	−0.17
III. Formal and informal sanctions	
Prison sentence imposed	0.04
Months of probation	−0.01
Fine imposed	0.72**
Lost job	−0.35
Bankruptcy	0.34
Family suffering	−0.39
Remorse	0.37

Table 6.2. *(cont.)*

Variable	Estimate
IV. Other variables	
Female	0.87***
Age at criterion offense	0.00
Non white	−0.46
Offense[a]	
Antitrust	−0.70
Bank embezzlement	−0.37
Bribery	−0.46
Credit fraud	−0.93*
False claims	−0.20
Mail fraud	−0.67
Securities	−1.34***
(tax)	

* Significant at $p < .05$;
** Significant at $p < .01$;
*** Significant at $p < .001$.
noncensored values = 251;
right censored values = 607;
log likelihood = −771.1.
[a] Where a variable is represented by a set of dummy variables, the excluded category is listed in parentheses. The overall significance of the variable is given opposite the category name. The significance of the differences between the individual dummy variables and the excluded category is given next to each dummy category.

model, time to failure, is the time to the first arrest after sentencing for the criterion offense.[8]

Of the variables that indicate social stability and achievement and more general deviance, only two are statistically significant in

[8] In our sample it is important to note that most people do not recidivate in the follow-up period, though the model estimated assumes that they would fail given an infinite tracking period.

our model: marital status and drug use. As predicted by prior criminal career studies, being married, increases the predicted time to failure. Involvement with illicit drugs, as in many studies of street criminals, acts to accelerate time to failure.

The effects of other indicators reflecting dimensions of social stability, ties to the community, and social position, are generally in the expected direction, though not statistically significant. For example, having a positive reputation in the community and being a homeowner increase the predicted time until failure in the sample, while having a reported alcohol problem or poor school performance decreases failure time. Similarly, as years of education increase, so does the predicted time until failure in the sample. Of the social class groupings, officers have the longest predicted time until failure.[9]

Consistent with prior criminal career studies, the number of arrests reported before the criterion offense has a strong and significant impact on recidivism. On average, when other variables in the model are held constant, offenders with more prior arrests recidivate more quickly than those with fewer prior arrests. While not statistically significant, the impact of "most serious prior offense" is also in the expected direction: Those who have committed more serious offenses have somewhat shorter times to failure in the sample.

Of the variables indicating the nature of formal sanctions imposed on offenders, neither prison nor probation has a statistically significant impact on time to failure. For prison, this result reinforces the findings reported in Chapter 5. It may be that probation has little impact, compared to other criminal career studies, because the average time to failure of members of the sample is much longer than the average probation sentence. It would follow in this case that most arrests are not a function of

---

[9] Reflecting a contrary relationship, having children decreases the time to failure in the sample – though only slightly. Of course, we remind the reader that the effects here as with the other variables discussed are not statistically significant. Accordingly, we cannot reliably rule out the possibility that the differences observed are due to chance sampling fluctuations.

the surveillance of probationers.[10] Assuming that the average time to rearrest is strongly correlated with the average time to reoffending itself, increased surveillance in the short run may have much less impact on official criminal careers in a white-collar crime sample than in other crime samples.

While prison and probation penalties do not strongly influence recidivism in this model, the imposition of a fine does. On average, those offenders who are fined fail later than other offenders in the sample, and this relationship is statistically significant. The most straightforward explanation for this finding is that fines have a particular importance for people convicted of white-collar crimes. In this regard, it is reasonable to assume that economic sanctions are generally more consequential for white-collar criminals than for others. The dollar amount of fines in the sample, while often small relative to the offenses themselves, are not trivial,[11] and white-collar offenders are typically much more likely to have assets to lose than are those convicted of common crimes. Nonetheless, this would not necessarily explain why fines and not prison or probation have an impact on recidivism.

John Braithwaite (1989) suggests one potential reason why fines may be more effective than other more punitive sanctions. He argues that sanctions may work best in circumstances in which the offender is able to reintegrate into the community after being punished. Prison and probation sanctions, particularly for white-collar offenders, may hinder such reintegration. The stigma of imprisonment or criminal justice supervision through probation can have an impact both upon the self-image of the offender and upon the ways in which he or she is viewed by neighbors,

---

[10] Months of probation imposed range from 0 to 60. Approximately 17% of the offenders were sentenced to more than 60 months' probation; these values were rounded down to 60 for purposes of estimating the model.

[11] The mean fine imposed for the criterion offense was $6,250 (median, $3,000). It should be kept in mind that the fines were imposed in the late 1970s. In today's dollars the sums would be equivalent to about 2.5 times the original fines imposed (American Institute for Economic Research, 1999).

friends, and family. Prison in particular, with its withdrawal of the offender from the community, is often assumed to have long-lasting effects on the ability of offenders to reestablish conventional ties. In comparison, fines neither remove the offender from the community nor affect the activities of the offender in the community. Indeed, an imposed fine, unlike a prison sentence, might go unnoticed by friends and neighbors. Fines, therefore, may represent a consequential sanction for white-collar criminals that at the same time does not inhibit successful reintegration of the offender.[12]

None of the measures of informal or secondary sanctions have a statistically significant effect on the time to failure. We conclude, accordingly, that collateral consequences of punishment are not major factors influencing rearrest for those convicted of white-collar crimes. It is clear, however, that the relationships observed in the sample are complex. For example, while a personal or business bankruptcy recorded at the time of sentencing increases the predicted failure time in the sample, losing a job as a result of an offense decreases the predicted failure time. At the same time, the expression of remorse about an offense is associated with an increase in the predicted time until failure in the sample, and family suffering is associated with a decrease in predicted time until failure. These results are not statistically significant and thus should not be overstated because they could simply be the result of chance sampling fluctuations. However, they may reflect the complex interplay of a number of factors including potential deterrent, backfire, and stigmatization effects of sanctions, as well

[12] Gordon and Glaser (1991) suggest a similar conclusion in their study of financial penalties imposed in municipal courts in California. They find that jail sentences lead to higher rates of recidivism as compared with probation and fines. While the differences between probation and fine sentences in regard to recidivism outcomes are not statistically significant, they argue that they are consistent enough that "there is some suggestion of beneficial effects" of fines. They conclude that fines may be a punishment that is punitive enough "to be salient to the individual" but not so punitive that it "produces negative consequences, such as loss of employment" (Gordon and Glaser, 1991, p. 672).

as the dynamic interaction of attitudes toward illegitimate behaviors and access to opportunities for both offending and conformity (Waring et al., 1995).

Of the demographic and background variables, only gender has a significant effect on the predicted time until rearrest. As in common crime samples, men are predicted to recidivate more quickly than women. However, the relative importance of gender in this model is somewhat greater than that found in other criminal career studies. Gender is the most significant and most strongly predictive variable included in the analysis. One explanation for its importance is simply that the proportion of women in this sample is larger than that found in most criminal career studies, thus greatly enhancing the sensitivity of the analysis.

It is reasonable to speculate, however, that situational components of offending, reflecting broad opportunity structures, are also relevant to these findings. Feeley (1996) argues that the assumption that women are unlikely to be involved in serious crime is a relatively modern one. Two centuries ago, women made up a much higher proportion of those found in the criminal courts and prisons than they do today. He suggests that the factors that have most influenced the low rates of female offending in contemporary times are variation in controls over women and in the opportunities available to them in employment and society more generally. Women may simply confront fewer worthwhile opportunities for criminality. These opportunities may be even more limited for the generally middle-class women in this sample than for the lower-class women typically found in samples of street criminals.[13]

None of the other variables have strong effects on recidivism. Although whites in the sample have a predicted failure time that is somewhat longer than others, the effect of race is not statistically significant. Age also fails to emerge as a significant effect in

---

[13] While generally "middle class," it should be noted that the women in this sample are, on average, of somewhat lower status than the men (see Daly, 1989). For example, the women bank employees are most often clerical workers, while the men are more likely to be loan officers or managers.

the model. However, it should be kept in mind that the lognormal model we use assumes that the risk of rearrest will, after an initial period, decrease over time. Therefore the model itself assumes that risk will decrease with the aging of a specific individual. Finally, in contrast to findings related to other aspects of the criminal process (see Weisburd et al., 1991), the statutory category of the criterion offense did not have a statistically significant effect on recidivism.

The Changing Risks of Recidivism over Time

While examination of predicted time until failure is a useful way to understand the effect that a specific variable has on the risk of recidivism, it is not the only approach to understanding this issue. An alternative method of interpretation is to examine the probability that an offender who is at risk at the beginning of a specific time interval will fail during that interval (e.g., the probability that a person who survives year 1 will fail during year 2). This function is also known as the hazard function. A hazard of 0 indicates 0 risk of failure in the time period identified. The hazard function provides a better understanding of the ways that different values of an independent variable lead to differences in predicted recidivism and how those differences change with the passage of time. For each of the variables found statistically significant in the multivariate time to failure analysis, we examine the observed annual hazard of rearrest.[14]

Figure 6.1 depicts the observed annual hazard rates for those who are married, single, or formerly married. As is illustrated in the figure, the differences between those who are married and others is largest in the period immediately after the criterion offense and then continues to decrease throughout the follow-up period. For example, the hazard for those married in the 12th month of follow-up is about .003, while the hazard for those who were single is about .011. By six years into the follow-up period

[14] We use the annualized hazard because it shows patterns over time well and provides a good balance between too much and too little detail.

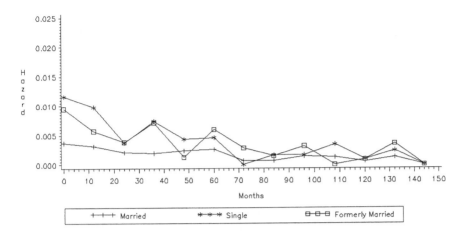

Figure 6.1. Observed annual hazard rates by marital status.

the difference between the groups has halved, and by ten years the hazards are nearly identical.

A similar relationship is found for drug use, though the differences between the groups are larger at the outset, and they decline much more quickly (see Figure 6.2). In the first month of follow-up the hazard for drug-involved offenders is about .018, while for those not involved in drugs the hazard is .005. By six years into the follow-up period the difference in hazards between the two groups has virtually disappeared.

Figure 6.3 shows the hazards for those with no prior arrests, two prior arrests, and seven or more prior arrests.[15] As can be seen in the figure, the largest gaps between the groups again occur at the very outset of the follow-up period. As with drug use, the difference in hazards between those with no prior arrests and those with two prior arrests becomes negligible by the time half of the follow-up period has passed. Interestingly, however, for the highest-rate offenders, the impacts appear to last throughout the

[15] We use 7 or more priors in this graph, rather than 11 or more (the upper limit in earlier chapters), in order to allow a large enough number of cases to reasonably illustrate the time-to-failure distribution.

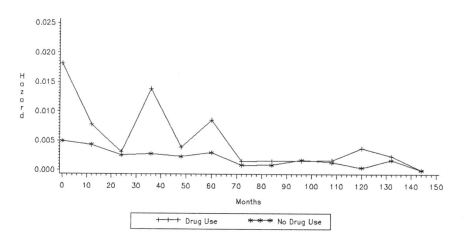

Figure 6.2. Observed annual hazard rates by drug use.

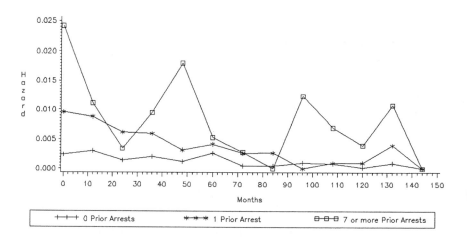

Figure 6.3. Observed annual hazard rates by number of prior arrests.

follow-up period. This finding is consistent with the discussion in Chapter 4, which noted that the highest-rate offenders were more likely to fit the image of stereotypical criminals. The analysis here, similarly, suggests that offenders with high-frequency criminal records are likely to show evidence of consistent involvement in crime across long periods in their lives.

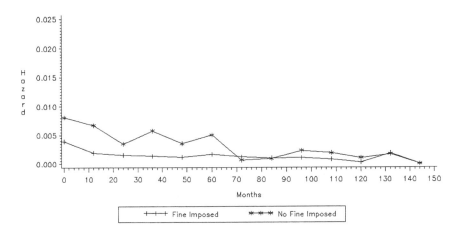

Figure 6.4. Observed annual hazard rates by imposed fine.

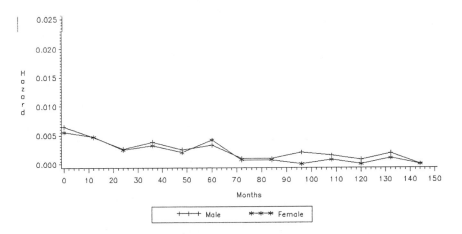

Figure 6.5. Observed annual hazard rates by gender.

For fines, fairly constant differences are found in the first six years after the criterion offense (see Figure 6.4). Then, following the pattern of the other measures, the effect observed nearly disappears. In contrast to the other relationships examined, the hazard rates for gender are more consistent over time, with men generally having a higher hazard than women (see Figure 6.5).

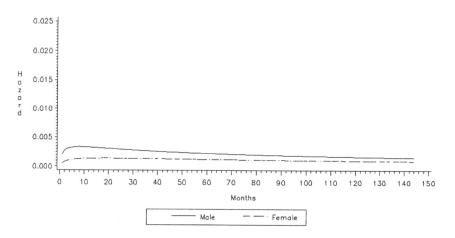

Figure 6.6. Predicted annual hazard rates by gender.

However, the differences between men and women do not appear large. In this figure, the observed hazards give a somewhat misleading view of the impacts of gender. This is the case because gender effects, unlike effects of other factors examined, are strongest when other variables are taken into account.[16] Looking at the predicted hazards in Figure 6.6, which are based on monthly estimates from the multivariate accelerated failure time model described earlier, the strength and consistency of the gender effect is more clearly illustrated.

Implications for Understanding Criminal Careers

These analyses lead to two general conclusions about the criminal careers of convicted white-collar offenders. The first is simply that factors that have been found to contribute to recidivism in street crime also contribute to recidivism in white-collar crime. Those who are unmarried, have a history of drug use, have

[16] Of the five statistically significant variables from the multivariate model, only gender has no statistically significant bivariate relationship with time to failure.

a more lengthy prior record, and are men, are likely to be rearrested more quickly in our study, as in studies of street crime offenders. While we find differences in the relative weight of such factors – for example, gender is more important in predicting rearrest in our study while prior drug use is less important – our finding supports those who argue that there are common underlying causes of both white-collar crime and more common types of offending (Hirschi and Gottfredson, 1987; Sutherland, 1940, 1949).

Our second conclusion confirms our findings in earlier chapters and is consistent with what is known about recidivism in studies of street criminals. It is difficult to predict future criminality on the basis of knowledge of the offenders past social and criminal conduct and circumstances.[17] While a wide range of measures reflecting social conventionality and achievement, deviance, and prior criminality were examined, only a handful were found to have significant impacts on rearrest. It might of course be the case that were we to have a fuller portrait of the offender and his or her circumstances at the time of the criterion offense, such as that which might be gained in a self-report study, we would be able to predict recidivism with much greater success. Nonetheless, we think that it is important that so many of the variables that might be expected to influence future rearrest do not.

Moreover, even those variables that evidence a statistically significant impact upon recidivism are not likely to sustain their effects on recidivism in the long run. This observation is particularly important for the types of recidivism documented in this sample. As discussed in Chapter 5, the average time to failure for those who are rearrested in our study is very long, and most offenders did not fail in the follow-up period. The predicted

---

[17] For discussions of the difficulty of predicting recidivism more generally, see Albrecht and Moitra (1988), Barnett and Lofaso (1985), Blumstein and Cohen (1978), Elliott et al. (1987), Estrich et al. (1983), and Gottfredson and Gottfredson (1992). For a discussion of a case with somewhat more success in prediction, see Schmidt and Witte, (1988).

median time to rearrest based on our multivariate model is more than ten years. This means that the influence of the variables that have the largest effect on time to failure are likely to become inconsequential just when many white-collar offenders are at the highest risk of rearrest.

Conclusions

When Edwin Sutherland first introduced the concept of white-collar crime, he sought to add complexity and generality to theories of crime that were all too often focused on a particular type of offender and circumstance. Certainly, he argued, it is incorrect to see crime as a problem unique to the poor and disadvantaged if it can be found in well-off neighborhoods and among those who live in situations of authority and privilege. Obviously, the harms of major stock frauds and the creation of illegal trusts have more long-term impact than the petty offenses of most street criminals. But Sutherland hoped to do more than debunk what had seemed certain about the origins or characteristics of criminality. For Sutherland, the identification of white-collar crime was meant to provide substantive contributions to our understanding of crime, criminality, and the criminal justice system.

In studying the criminal careers of convicted white-collar offenders we have taken an approach consistent with Sutherland's original intention of using the white-collar crime category to explore more general questions in the study of crime and justice. In this concluding chapter, we want to focus directly on three main areas where our work has raised new concerns or intriguing questions. We begin by exploring the ways in which our description of criminal careers in a white-collar crime sample challenges traditional stereotypes of criminals and criminality. We then turn to the implications of our study for understanding involvement in crime. We focus particular attention on the importance of situational, as contrasted with historical, explanations for criminal behavior. Finally, we examine how our data lead us to reconsider common assumptions about the role of criminal justice sanctions in altering the nature or form of criminal careers. Having summarized the major themes of our work, we close the chapter with our thoughts about the policy implications of our study.

Crime and Criminality

When lay people use the term criminality, or when they call people criminals, they are not simply referring to the fact that someone has come into contact with the criminal justice system. Criminality has a much broader meaning. Like nationality, culture, or religion, the criminal label is intended to convey a great deal about those to whom it is applied. Criminals are generally viewed as dangerous to society, as products of bad genes or bad parenting or broken communities. Crime is not merely an incident in such peoples' lives. The criminal label summarizes a vast array of behaviors and activities, and it communicates something very meaningful about who such people are and where they are going. Most importantly, criminals are different.[1] This is a very comfortable moral position, and one that helps the rest of us to define what we have in common with each other.

The lay view of criminality is reflected in the interests of professional criminologists. Almost from the outset, scholars concerned with crime and justice have sought to identify those characteristics of offenders that set them apart from ordinary law-abiding citizens (Gabor, 1994). Of course, in searching for the characteristics that make criminals different, criminologists have accepted, in some sense, the view that criminals are indeed different in the first place. The choice of subject reflects the basic theoretical assumptions of this approach. In looking to identify

[1] Marcus Felson refers to this perspective as the "not-me fallacy," arguing that most people would like to believe that they are "fundamentally" different from serious offenders (Felson, 1998, p. 10).

CONCLUSIONS

the factors that distinguish criminals from noncriminals, criminologists have begun with theories that locate the causes of crime in the biological, personal, or social histories of offenders.

Many of the predominant themes in this criminological perspective can be traced to the founding generations of criminology in the nineteenth century. Lombroso (1911), for example, looked for the origins of criminality in the physical characteristics of the criminals he studied. He stressed that the "anti-social tendencies of criminals are the result of their physical and psychic organization, which differs essentially from that of normal individuals" (Lombroso, 1911, p. 5). A series of other nineteenth-century scholars concerned with crime noted differences in the economic, social, and religious characteristics of geographic areas, and they also noted the relationship of these factors to official crime rates (e.g., see Durkheim, 1897; Guerry, 1833; Quetelet, 1835). In one sense, this view of the correlates of crime was not so much focused on the factors that differentiate offenders from others as with identifying areas where crime is more common. However, criminologists have generally used these broader social characteristics to identify factors that lead individuals to crime.

For example, the important insights related to crime and social disorganization brought by University of Chicago sociologists in the 1920s and 1930s (e.g., Thrasher, 1927; Shaw and McKay, 1931, 1942) are often translated into correlates of individual criminality. The idea that areas where social control is weak are breeding grounds for crime became part of a more general theory of criminality in which criminals are regarded as the products of broken neighborhoods and broken families. They are different from others because of the defects found in their upbringings and circumstances, not in their genes. Still, criminals continued to be considered different from others, and these differences were identified as the keys to understanding criminality.

In distinguishing elements of the prior experiences, social backgrounds, and development of offenders that produce criminality, criminologists have advanced a diverse group of theories and perspectives that are too numerous to mention here. But it is fair to say that whether the focus has been on factors such as anomie (Merton, 1938; see also Adler and Laufer, 1995; Passas and Agnew, 1997), social control (e.g., Hirschi, 1969), social learning (e.g., Akers, 1996, 1998; Sutherland and Cressey, 1960), or culture (e.g., Miller, 1958), there is a common theme in much criminological theory that looks to the offender and his or her past to gain an understanding of involvement in crime. The idea of criminality is one of process and history, in which specific characteristics of offenders and their environments lead them almost inevitably to criminality. Moreover, its portrait of offending often fits a morality play, in which the first acts, representing the first years of an offender's life, lead to an inevitable decline into deviance and criminality.

Even more recent perspectives which recognize that offenders, like others, will change and develop as a response to life course events and experiences begin with an assumption that there is something unique to the development of offenders that explains their participation in crime. Robert Sampson and John Laub (1993), for example, in their book *Crime in the Making* look to develop a comprehensive theory to explain the varied pathways to crime that are found in childhood, adolescence, and adulthood. They argue that some offenders will evidence continuity in deviant and antisocial behavior throughout the life course. Others will end their criminal careers as a result of "salient life events and socialization experiences in adulthood" (Sampson and Laub, 1993, p. 246). Still others will initiate involvement in crime in adulthood as a consequence of weak social bonds, such as weak labor force or marital attachments. But even while recognizing that paths to crime may begin at different stages of an offender's life, scholars taking this approach identify in every stage specific influences that increase (or decrease) the propensity of offenders to participate in crime and other deviant behaviors in the future. The causes of crime remain rooted in the factors that differentiate offenders from others.

One challenge to the traditional idea of criminality was brought by advocates of the societal reaction approach to deviance (e.g., Becker, 1963; Erikson, 1962; Kitsuse, 1962). These scholars began with a radical critique of conventional theories. In explaining the causes of crime, they emphasized the reactions of society rather than the nature of offenders themselves. Again, this approach may be traced to nineteenth-century criminology, especially to Emile Durkheim's (1895) theories of the functionality of deviance for society. Societal reaction theorists did not assume that criminals began as different from others. Indeed, building on self-report studies which showed a very broad range of offending among people without criminal records (e.g., see Short and Nye, 1958; Wallerstein and Wyle, 1947), they argued that what differentiated criminals from others was simply the fact that they were labeled as such (e.g., see Erikson, 1962).

But this fact once again becomes a very important part of defining the ways in which criminals are different from noncriminals. Even if the fault lies with the societal reaction, the criminal, once labeled, is seen to fall into a spiral of deviance and related social problems (Wilkins, 1965). The criminal in this case begins much like others, but becomes different once labeled, fulfilling society's image of what the criminal should be like.

Another challenge to the moralistic view of criminals and criminality was initiated by crime prevention scholars in England (Clarke, 1980, 1983; Clarke and Cornish, 1985). In part because of the seeming failures of offender-centered crime prevention strategies (e.g., see Lipton et al., 1975; Martinson, 1974; Sechrest et al., 1979), these theorists began to explore the importance of situational opportunities in the development of crime. They called for a more crime-specific and situational approach to crime, focusing less on the offender than on the opportunities available in specific situations. Many advocates of this approach adopted a perspective on crime which emphasized rational choice in the identification of criminal targets and the decision to commit crimes (e.g., see Cornish and Clarke, 1986).

Nonetheless, situational crime prevention advocates did not stake out a clear position on either the idea of criminality or the implications of their approach for the traditional distinctions made between offenders and nonoffenders (Clarke, 1999). They sought more generally to offset the imbalance in criminological theory, which had neglected the crime situation and the importance of opportunities for crime in favor of asking "why certain people might be more criminally inclined or less so" (Felson and

Clarke, 1998, p. 1). Their approach did not demand a radical restructuring of traditional images of criminality, but rather that situational opportunities be given greater weight in understanding and preventing crime. Moreover, in their efforts to reorient crime prevention policies, situational prevention scholars naturally placed the question of criminality in the background, and they focused their primary interest on the problem of how opportunities for crime may be blocked in specific situations (Weisburd, 1997).

Even the emphasis on rational choice that is often part of situational crime prevention approaches does not necessarily require that perspectives that emphasize distinctions between criminals and noncriminals be abandoned. Offenders' assessments of the costs and benefits of criminal behavior are often considered to be different from those of ordinary people (Cornish and Clarke, 1986). Their particular commitment to crime may lead them to weigh costs and benefits differently. Weak social bonds, social instability, and inability to delay gratification may in this context also be seen as impacting upon the processes that underlie the rational choices of offenders to take advantage of criminal opportunities (Hirschi and Gottfredson, 1986). In theory, situational prevention does not require that offenders differ at all from nonoffenders. In practice, however, many situational crime prevention researchers continue to accept traditional assumptions about criminality.

A major goal of our research was to examine the extent to which offenders convicted of white-collar crimes would challenge this comfortable view of criminals as different from others in society. While theorists concerned with crime have more often than not ignored white-collar criminals, those who have taken this category into account have typically assumed that these offenders have pathways to crime that are similar to other criminals, even if their circumstances are very different (e.g., see Sutherland, 1940; Hirschi and Gottfredson, 1987). For example, Gottfredson and Hirschi argue in their book *A General Theory of Crime* (1990, p. 200) that the characteristics of individuals committing crime are similar regardless of the types of crimes they commit. They assert that "crime in the street and crime in the suite is an offense rather than an offender distinction" and that "offenders in both cases are likely to share similar characteristics." For Hirschi and Gottfredson (1987, pp. 959–960), as well as many other criminologists, those characteristics set the offender apart from the rest of us:

> . . . criminality is the tendency of individuals to pursue short-term gratification in the most direct way with little consideration for the long term consequences of their acts (Indicators of such a tendency include impulsivity, aggression, activity level, and lack of concern for the opinion of others). . . . [P]eople high on this tendency are relatively indifferent to punishment and to the interests of others. As a consequence, they tend to be impulsive, active and risk taking.

Do convicted white-collar crime offenders exhibit traits that are associated with more traditional criminal populations? While of higher social class, do white-collar criminals evidence significant degrees of social instability, short-sightedness, inability to delay gratification, impulsiveness, and a series of other characteristics often associated with criminality? Or can we say that for white-collar crime, criminals are not very different from other people in similar social and economic circumstances who do not have contact with the criminal justice system?

Our study does not provide a single answer to these questions. We do identify offenders in our sample, those we have termed stereotypical criminals, who fit stereotypes of criminality. Their social and criminal records are consistent with common images of the criminal. However, most of those we study do not fit easily into conventional understandings. Irrespective of their involvement in crime, their lives do not appear to be very different from those of law-abiding citizens. For those termed opportunity takers and crisis responders, the notion of a progression into crime and deviance belies what is most important about their involvement in the criminal justice system: Such involvement is often an aberration on a record that is otherwise characterized by conventionality and not by deviance.

Even many of those in our sample who have more serious criminal records depart markedly from common stereotypes of criminality. These offenders were labeled opportunity seekers. On the one hand, their social and criminal records suggest that their crimes are not aberrations on unblemished records. Instead, they are part of a pattern of behavior that often reaches into childhood and that sometimes leads to a lifetime of scheming and fraud. On the other hand, these criminals still evidence many characteristics of conformity and stability that are generally not associated with criminality.

Some scholars would argue that white-collar crime is interesting precisely because it is a deviant case. In this sense, our findings might be regarded as a reinforcement of what is conventionally believed about white-collar criminals: They are so different from other offenders that little can be learned from their experiences about the more general problem of crime. Study of white-collar crime, in this context, represents an interesting though esoteric enterprise.

While our results are gained from a sample of convicted white-collar criminals, we believe that they have broader implications for the study of crime. In the most basic sense, many individuals who are convicted for common crimes are similar to white-collar criminals in that they do not show evidence of a criminal career. Although the study of criminal careers has largely focused on chronic offenders, it has long been recognized that lower-frequency offenders comprise a large part of the criminal population (e.g., see Blumstein et al., 1986). Petersilia (1980), for example, observes that more than half of all offenders with one official contact with the police will never have another (see also Tillman, 1987). While rearrest rates are much higher for those who are convicted of crimes, and even higher for those who have served prison sentences (e.g., see Maltz, 1984; Schmidt and Witte, 1988), a substantial portion of those who experience arrest, conviction, and even imprisonment will have only one or a very small number of contacts with the criminal justice system.

It is possible that infrequent contacts with the criminal justice system belie otherwise deviant and unconventional lifestyles. These offenders may conform to many of the stereotypes of criminality that we have discussed. However, we suspect that in common crime samples, as in our sample, many such people do not differ very much from others in their communities who are not identified and processed by the criminal justice system.[2]

Our decision to examine criminal careers in a white-collar crime sample led us to a focus on types of offenders that are often ignored in other studies. This approach leads us to abandon, at least in part, the moralistic view of criminality that has drawn the public's imagination and is reflected in much criminological theory. Criminals may often be just like others in the community. Their criminality may reveal little more than that they have committed a crime. This may be a less satisfying position for some than perspectives that attempt to distinguish offenders from nonoffenders, but it is relevant to large numbers of people who participate in crime.

The Relevance of Situational Attitudes and Opportunities

Having argued that traditional distinctions made between offenders and nonoffenders are often more reflective of society's moralistic approach to the crime problem than the reality of crimes and criminals, we are led to the second major theme of our work. For many criminals, the key to understanding involvement in crime is not found in their distant pasts or in the complexities of human development. Rather it lies in the immediate context of the crimes that they commit.

Situation plays a central role in explaining participation in crime for most offenders in this sample.[3] The lives of those we

[2] Support for our position comes in part from street crime studies that have contrasted offenders with less and more serious criminal records. In general it is reported that less chronic offenders are less likely to evidence traits of instability and deviance than are chronic offenders. Of course, this does not directly address the question of whether such offenders are similar to nonoffenders in comparable social and economic circumstances.

[3] It is important to note that our study also supports specific elements of perspectives that emphasize the importance of life course events in understanding crime. For example, the emphasis on adult

have termed opportunity takers and crisis responders do not seem to be characterized by instability and deviance, and there was little in their records that indicated a predisposition to criminality. Indeed, there was frequently evidence to the contrary. A specific crisis or special opportunity appears to have drawn otherwise conventional people across the line to crime. Even for those described as opportunity seekers, situational opportunities play an important role in defining why offenders commit crimes at specific junctures.

While theorists concerned with the personal attributes associated with criminality have sometimes recognized the relevance of situational characteristics of crime (e.g., see Gottfredson and Hirschi, 1990), they are primarily interested in the offender and not the crime situation. For our sample, however, understanding criminality best begins not with the characteristics of individuals but rather with the situations in which crimes occur. But how can such criminality be understood? Is it plausible to suggest that individuals will suddenly become involved in crime and then, just as suddenly, return to conventional lifestyles and careers?

Many of these white-collar criminals maintain positive attitudes toward conventionality and legality even while participating in crime. Many of those labeled crisis responders are, by and large, conformists, but, in a specific situation, they feel the need to do something they define as wrong in order to deal with some perceived crisis that threatens them, their families, or their companies. Even when committing crime, they accept the fact that they should conform to legal norms, but believe they cannot.

People we have defined as opportunity takers also accept more generally legal and conventional norms. Arguably, such people

---

development and informal social controls in the work place of Sampson and Laub (1993) is confirmed in our finding of the consistent importance of marital status in understanding criminal histories. Nonetheless, what is most striking in our work is the degree to which attributes of the offender's prior social record fail to provide very much insight into his or her involvement in crime. Of course, as noted in earlier chapters, this could be a result of limitations in our data rather than the causal processes that underlie offending.

would not have violated the law in the first place if a specific opportunity had not confronted them. Although they do not seek out such criminal opportunities, once they appear, opportunity takers decide that conventional norms are holding them up in a specific circumstance. Thus even when becoming involved in crime, both crisis responders and opportunity takers maintain their commitment to conventionality. The crimes they commit appear as aberrations on otherwise law-abiding records.

Of course, it is still the case that these criminals have made the decision at that situational juncture to become involved in crime. They might, in contrast, have decided not to take advantage of a specific criminal opportunity or to have responded with conventional rather than criminal behavior to a specific crisis in their lives. This line of reasoning implies that there is a specific moral decision that is made before each criminal act. Clearly, different people might respond differently in such circumstances, and individual personality traits are likely to influence the decisions made.

The question for criminologists and others interested in understanding crime is whether it is possible to identify these traits systematically. If they are peculiar to each individual's development, then they offer little assistance in the prediction of criminal involvement. For many criminals in our sample it is very difficult to identify characteristics that help to unravel their choice to become involved in crime. Such causes may be so individualistic and varied, and found in such different places over the life course, that it is virtually impossible for scholars to identify them or for public policy makers to use them to develop crime prevention policies. The causes of criminality in this context may be similar to the causes of changes in our weather or other phenomena for which long-range forecasts are difficult. The chain of causal events involves so many factors that can have such varied effects that reliable long-term prediction at the individual level becomes virtually impossible.

It need not be assumed, however, that the white-collar criminals we study are distinguishable from those who do not commit crime by the ways in which they make situational choices about criminal involvement. It may be that, at some point, most people allow deviations from what is otherwise considered acceptable behavior. This position is taken, for example, by Thomas Gabor (1994), in his provocative book, *Everybody Does It!* (see also Felson, 1998). Gabor (1994, p. 12) argues "that most, if not all, of us break laws, formal rules, and other social conventions at some point." In this context, we might speculate that many people would make decisions similar to those of the offenders we study when confronted with similar circumstances.

Mordechai Nisan, a scholar concerned with moral development, has coined the term "limited morality," to recognize that most people will, under specific circumstances, allow themselves to violate norms that they accept as legitimate (Nisan, 1985, 1991; Nisan and Horenczyk, 1990):

> ... when faced with a moral conflict, people do not aspire to be saints but rather allow themselves a measure of deviation from what they consider proper behaviour. Such deviation would not stem, therefore, from lack of knowledge or a distorted view of the right behaviour (e.g., neutralization of the deviation: Sykes and Matza, 1957), nor would it stem from weakness of will or an inability to resist temptation. The leeway a person gives him/herself to deviate from the right course may be a considered decision guided by principal. (Nisan and Horenczyk, 1990, p. 29)

To explain the decision to deviate, Nisan proposes a model of "moral balance," in which individuals weigh moral considerations against "nonmoral considerations" in deciding whether to violate a specific rule. Financial pressures, personal crises, or unusual opportunities all fall within the boundaries of nonmoral considerations. Violation of norms in this context does not imply that the individual has been improperly socialized or has a predisposition to rule breaking. This model appears particularly appropriate for those in our sample who argue that a specific crisis or opportunity has led them to violate the law.

Our emphasis on the situational components of criminal careers is consistent with data drawn from a sample of convicted white-collar criminals. However, the notion that situations play a central role in the development of crime is not unique to white-collar offenders. Indeed, the situational crime prevention approach discussed earlier in the chapter has been applied primarily to common crimes such as burglary, prostitution, auto theft, and robbery (Poyner, 1993; Clarke, 1992, 1995). But our approach does not simply recognize the importance of the crime situation in explaining a criminal event; we argue that for many criminals, situational components of crisis and opportunity are in fact the main explanations for their involvement in crime. While this issue is not generally addressed in situational prevention studies, a similar approach is suggested by Felson and Clarke (1998) in an article entitled "Opportunity Makes the Thief."[4]

Finally, we think that it is important to recognize that the situational causes of crime we observe in our sample may not be relevant for other crime samples. For common crime offenders, other considerations may have more significance. For example, Donald Black (1983, p. 34) contends that much common crime is a form of social control:

> There is a sense in which conduct regarded as criminal is often quite the opposite. Far from being an intentional violation of a prohibition, much crime is moralistic and involves the pursuit of justice. It is a mode of conflict management, possibly a form of punishment, even capital punishment. . . . To the degree that it defines or responds to the conduct of someone else – the victim – as deviant, crime is social control.

Crimes that involve retribution for offenses against family members, that result from disputes over property or rights, or that are aimed to punish others would all fall under this general rubric. Black (1983, p. 42) argues, as we have here, that it is often not useful to try to identify "how criminals differ from other people." His approach, like ours for white-collar crime, suggests that more is often learned by examining how specific situations lead otherwise law-abiding people to participate in crime.

[4] It is interesting to note that Felson and Clarke (1998, p. 2) use similar language to Nisan in discussing the idea "that opportunities cause crime." In discussing "experiments in temptation," they note that the findings indicate "that a person makes a *considered decision* whether to respond to temptation."

The Impacts of Criminal Sanctions

One implication of our emphasis on crisis and opportunity is that crimes committed by people in our sample often involve decision-making processes that are, within their context and in the understanding of the offender, reasoned. In this sense, the offenders we study appear to follow a rational choice model of offending (Cornish and Clarke, 1986). In such models, offenders are assumed to seek benefit in criminal behavior and weigh costs and benefits before deciding on involvement in crime. If this is the case, then our finding that a prison sentence does not influence rearrest seems contradictory. If our offenders are making rational choices, wouldn't we expect that a sentence of imprisonment would lead them to reconsider involvement in crime in the future?

In placing this finding in context, it is important to recognize that imprisonment may have very important impacts on other aspects of the lives of these criminals. For example, it seems likely that incarceration would influence the occupational or personal situations of offenders (see Waring et al., 1995), though, of course, criminal history records provide little information about these central features of their lives. Sampson and Laub (1993) argue, in this regard, that imprisonment does not have a direct impact on reoffending, but rather indirectly influences criminality through its effects on such factors as occupational and marital stability. Other studies suggest that criminal justice interventions that are deemed failures in terms of recidivism may have significant influence on quality of life, as measured by employment or personal stability of the offenders studied (Berk et al., 1980; Rossi et al., 1980).

One plausible explanation for our finding that prison sentences have little impact on future arrests is that the maximum deterrent value of criminal justice punishment has already been gained by the time the offender has been sentenced. A short prison stay, the main type of sanction imposed in our sample, may not provide more than a marginal impact beyond the experience of arrest, prosecution, and conviction. In this sense, our offenders may be responding to punishment, but are affected most by punishments that derive from earlier experiences with the criminal justice system.

Many observers of the criminal justice system believe that movement through the legal process takes a greater toll on white-collar criminals than on other criminals. Indeed, some scholars suggest that the effects of criminal justice processing are more consequential for the white-collar offender than the actual legal penalties they face after sentencing (e.g., see Benson, 1982). This is also a perception expressed by judges who sentence white-collar offenders (Wheeler, Mann, and Sarat, 1988). As one federal judge, interviewed in a companion investigation to the Yale study from which our data are drawn, argued:

> There is no doubt about the fact that in most white-collar crimes as such the return of the indictment is much more traumatic than even the sentence. Pronouncing of the sentence is not as injurious to the person, his relationship to the community, to his family, as the return of the indictment. The return of the indictment in many instances causes a tremendous loss, is felt, the loss of business relationships, often the loss of jobs, of bank credit, a loss of friends, social status, occasionally loss of a wife, members of the family, children around the father, more when they hear that an indictment has been returned and he has been charged than they do after they have gotten used to the idea and he is sentenced for it. (Wheeler, Mann, and Sarat, 1988, p. 145)

The toll of the criminal justice process is often alluded to in the presentence investigations. Many offenders appear to be sincerely shocked at what has befallen them, and they often make statements expressing this shock to the probation officers. Of course, as noted earlier, such statements may be part of a strategy to draw sympathy from judges at time of sentencing. Nonetheless, they have a ring of truth to them, which appears often to have persuaded the probation officers as well. Take, for example, the account of a bribery offender also convicted of perjury as quoted in the presentence investigation:

> Regretfully, I did not tell the Grand Jury the complete truth of the matter. Under the stress and panic I was under I could not remember the details and facts as I ordinarily would. Even to the fact that

immediately after leaving the Grand Jury, I called my wife at her place of employment and asked if I could speak to Mrs. ———, her previously married name. . . . I will regret this action for the rest of my life. These past six months have been a living hell not only for me but for my wife and those closely associated with me.

One explanation for the failure of imprisonment sanctions to have greater impact on future arrests thus may develop from the already salient impacts of prosecution and conviction. But this argument does not take into account the fact that we do find a statistically significant impact of fines on recidivism, even after other factors such as imprisonment and probation have been taken into account. Clearly, there is room for additional deterrence, even if we agree that much of the deterrent value of punishment has come from experiences earlier in the criminal justice process.

Gordon and Glaser (1991) provide insight into this problem in a study of the effects of financial penalties in municipal courts in California. They found, overall, that relative to jail terms, probation and fines were associated with a lower likelihood of post-sentencing arrests, incarcerations, and probation revocations. Though they could not reliably distinguish between the impacts of fines and probation, they speculate on the relative effectiveness of fines as a criminal sanction. They draw from the work of Joan McCord (1985), who suggests the effectiveness of sanctions that express the "light touch of the law." They argue that fines may present "enough of a punishment to be salient to the individual, but not so much as to produce negative consequences" (Gordon and Glaser, 1991, p. 672).[5]

This argument, of course, is consistent with our discussion in Chapter 6, where we suggested that fines provide a consequential form of punishment that nonetheless allows reintegration into the community (see Braithwaite, 1989). As noted earlier, fines (in

[5] We need not assume in this regard that fines represent a less consequential form of punishment. See Posner (1980) for a theoretical discussion of the possibility that fines can be equal in severity to incarceration.

contrast to imprisonment) are not assumed to have long-lasting impacts on the ability of offenders to reestablish conventional ties. They do not remove the offender from the community, nor do they impact directly on the activities of the offender in the community. This may be one reason, in turn, why we do not find a significant impact of probation on recidivism in our sample. Probation, in contrast to fines, does directly impact on the activities of the offender during the period it is in force. The salience of fines, in turn, suggests that our offenders are responsive to punishment as predicted by a rational choice model of offending.

Policy Implications

In drawing policy implications from an empirical study, it is important to recognize the difficulty of making generalizations about broad societal concerns from data that are limited to specific settings and circumstances. Nonetheless, in our study, as in others, the findings do not simply reflect on academic debate and scientific concerns. Our observations regarding the nature of offenders, in particular, raise questions about criminal justice policies and suggest directions for criminal justice practice.

Our study emphasizes that offenders are often not very different from others in similar social and economic circumstances. This view of criminals is very much at odds with the underlying assumptions that are behind much recent criminal justice policy. The public and many policy makers remain committed to an idea of criminality which separates saints from sinners and also places a clear boundary between criminals and the rest of us (Gabor, 1994). This view of criminality has, as discussed above, been reinforced by many scholars who have tried to identify what distinguishes criminals from others.

Of course, one implication of what we have defined as the moral drama of criminality is that criminals are defined by the public as outsiders. They are not simply neutral outsiders, they are outsiders who threaten the community and its values. Deviance theorists have long pointed out the functions of the criminal for reinforcing community solidarity and clarifying community norms (e.g., see Becker, 1963; Durkheim, 1895; Erikson,

1962). In defining the criminal we reinforce what the rest of us have in common with each other. As in other forms of conflict, in the common threat that criminals represent, we are all brought closer together (Coser, 1967; Simmel, 1964).

The threat of crime and the perception that criminals are easily distinguished from the rest of us combine to create a powerful justification for ever-increasing criminal justice punishments. Such policies often begin with the offender in the community, along with what the community and the police can do to prevent crime. There is, for example, a growing focus on quality of life offenses in most American cities (e.g., see Kelling and Coles, 1996). Such policies often test the constitutional boundaries of how police may restrict the movements and activities of citizens. While many such policies are justified by recent crime prevention theory and are attempts to empower communities in their efforts to control crime, they reflect, in a broader sense, a willingness on the part of Americans to tighten their control over offenders, even when such actions may limit traditional American freedoms. As one commentator on controlling crime in New York has observed, recent tough crime control policies sometimes appear to be a "zero sum game in which more safety for some means more oppression for others" (Weisberg, 1999, p. 18). Of course, it is assumed that limits on freedom will apply only to the class of Americans that are defined as criminals.

Recent American imprisonment policies reflect in even starker terms the new punitive policies of crime control. Over the last decade, prison populations have increased more than 100 percent (Gilliard, 1999). We now have more than 1.8 million Americans sitting in jails and prisons on an average day; this means that in some states Americans have begun to spend more money on prisons than on colleges (Ambrosio and Schiraldi, 1997). Many states and the federal government have instituted so-called "three strikes and you're out" laws, which demand that offenders be given long-term sentences after a set number of arrests, irrespective of the nature of the offender or the circumstances of his or her crimes (Shichor, 1997; Vitiello, 1997).

While the moral idea of criminality is not the only cause of such punitive punishment policies, we believe that common assumptions about the criminal have allowed Americans to support such policies. Would it be so easy to call for more intrusive surveillance and control policies if such policies were directed at those we see as part of our communities? If criminals are just like us, would we be so quick to imprison them? Would ever-increasing punishment policies receive such support if we believed that people like us could in specific circumstances also become offenders?

We suspect that the answer to these questions is no. And in this sense, our data have particular importance for rethinking recent punitive crime control policies. We recognize that many offenders do in fact fit common stereotypes. However, many other people who commit crime are not very different from people who do not. This is true for white-collar crime; and as noted above, we suspect also true for much common crime. We believe that recognition of this fact would lead policy makers and the public to think more cautiously before developing more intrusive strategies for cracking down on offenders in the streets and would raise important concerns about present imprisonment policies.

Moreover, our data suggest that there is good reason to consider alternative prevention and punishment policies. In particular, our finding that prison does not deter future offending, while financial penalties do, supports those who argue for placing greater emphasis on nonincarcerative sentencing policies (e.g., see Morris and Tonry, 1990). Such options may provide for more effective and less costly sentencing options. Our findings are particularly important in light of policies that have increased the severity of punishment for white-collar criminals (e.g., see U.S. Sentencing Commission, 1987). More white collar criminals are now being sentenced to prison than was the case in earlier decades (United States Sentencing Commission, 1991). Our analyses suggest that this policy will not help to prevent future offending on the part of those who are sanctioned. Indeed, if prison sanctions are substituted for financial penalties, it is entirely possible that recidivism among white-collar criminals will increase.

When Edwin Sutherland raised the problem of white-collar crime, he sought to inform our general understanding of crime and criminality. Our approach has followed this tradition. In examining white-collar crime and criminal careers, we have sought to raise broader questions related to crimes, criminals, and the criminal justice system. Our sample has focused our attention on a part of the criminal population that is often overlooked in studies of crime. Studying these offenders has led us to think much more carefully about stereotypes of criminality and about situational factors in the development of crime.

Both lay people and criminologists often ask why others become involved in criminality. This seems to be a natural approach when the criminal population is defined as different from the rest of the community. However, our data suggest that to understand many of those who commit crime, the view of criminality that sets offenders and nonoffenders apart must be abandoned. This position may be unfamiliar and may be less comfortable than the moral drama that ordinarily focuses attention on crimes and criminals. Nonetheless, it is consistent with a significant proportion of the crime and criminals in our society.

Appendix A: Detailed Information about the Sample

Eight specific federal offenses were chosen by Wheeler, Weisburd, and Bode (1988) for inclusion in the sample used in the Yale study of white-collar offenders that is the basis for the sample used in this book (see Table A.1). They are: securities fraud, antitrust violations, bribery, bank embezzlement, postal and wire fraud, false claims and statements, credit and lending institution fraud, and tax fraud. The nature of the actual offenses – which we refer to as the criterion offenses – included in each category are briefly described below. These descriptions are based on the second chapter of Weisburd et al. (1991), which provides more detailed descriptions and numerous examples of each offense.

The *antitrust* statute prohibits all contacts, conspiracies, and combinations in restraint of trade, and it also prohibits monopolies and attempts to monopolize. Most of the antitrust offenses in the sample fall into the former category. Several antitrust conspiracies lasted fifteen years or more, and almost all continued more than a year. Most antitrust cases involve a number of conspirators, including both individuals and organizations. They often have many victims who may be unaware that they have been victimized. Of the eight offense categories in the sample, antitrust cases have the highest average amounts of illegal gain and the most victims. While a small number of cases involve Fortune 500 companies, in general, the cases in this sample do not begin to

Table A.1. *Number of individuals in Weisburd et al. (1991) (W) and currently used sample (C), by offense and district*

	District																	
	Southern New York		Maryland		Northern Georgia		Northern Texas		Northern Illinois		Central California		Western Washington		Other federal districts		Total	
Offense	W	C	W	C	W	C	W	C	W	C	W	C	W	C	W	C	W	C
Bank embezzlement	30	25	29	22	22	21	30	27	30	18	30	25	30	25	0	0	201	163
Tax fraud	30	19	30	15	30	20	30	26	30	17	30	24	30	22	0	0	210	143
Credit fraud	30	23	6	6	22	17	30	26	16	12	30	15	24	20	0	0	158	119
Mail fraud	30	24	30	22	30	26	30	27	30	24	30	28	10	7	0	0	190	158
Securities fraud	87	55	0	0	0	0	5	3	1	1	32	22	1	1	99	73	225	155
False claims	30	17	8	7	25	18	24	19	14	12	30	25	26	21	0	0	157	119
Bribery	30	18	11	7	0	0	8	5	16	8	17	13	2	2	0	0	84	53
Antitrust	15	9	4	3	6	6	0	0	0	0	2	2	0	0	90	38	117	58
All white-collar crimes	282	190	118	82	135	108	157	133	137	92	201	154	123	98	189	111	1342	968

rival in size or economic impact those antitrust cases which receive the most coverage in the mass media. In contrast to these well-known cases, most of these offenses involve activities and victims within a specific location or region.

Securities frauds involve misrepresentation intended to trick unsuspecting victims into poor investment decisions. They often last for long periods and involve large amounts of money. Deception can take many forms; the statutes prohibit the use of "any device, scheme, or artifice to defraud" in the sale of securities, as well as participation in "any transaction, practice, or course of business which operated or would operate as a fraud or deceive the purchaser." Securities, as defined by the Securities and Exchange Commission, include any investment instrument, from shares in railroad tank cars to shares in publicly traded corporations.

There are two main types of securities offenses in the sample. In the first, offenders sell securities to individual investors for considerably more than their actual value. Usually this involves misrepresenting to investors the value of the stock being sold or the financial condition of the issuing corporation. The sales of leases in dry wells, shares of near-bankrupt corporations, and unregistered stock are all examples of this form of securities fraud. In the second, legitimate securities are used for illegal purposes. Insiders in the securities industry buy, sell, or otherwise use stocks at their true values, but the transactions themselves are illegal. Most convicted securities brokers involved in these offenses acted in the interests of their firms rather than for themselves directly. In the sample most securities frauds are complex and result in losses of large sums of money, but some are seemingly quite simple.

Bribery involves attempts to influence government officials (and occasionally people in federally regulated private industries) by private persons or organizations. Although the bribery statute covers both offering and accepting bribes, most bribery offenders in the sample are prosecuted for offering bribes, less than half of which were accepted. Most of the bribery offenses in the sample represent attempts to have rules bypassed or waived. A small number of offenders attempted to secure the continuing service of government employees, and these represent some of the more complex crimes in this offense category. There are only a few cases where an official was paid to expedite a transaction that would have eventually been completed anyway.

Bank embezzlement occurs when a person who is an officer, director, agent, or other employee of a bank commits an offense against it. The offenders in this category range from low-level clerical workers to high-ranking officers. Bank embezzlement cases usually follow one of two patterns. In the first there is manipulation of accounts that belong to an individual customer. In the second there is illegal activity involving money that belongs to the bank itself. Although bank embezzlement may be extremely complex and involve millions of dollars, it may also be committed in a fashion closely resembling simple theft. Of all of the offenses included in the sample, bank embezzlements have the lowest average level of illegal gain and the smallest number of victims.

Mail and wire fraud covers the widest variety of wrongs of the offenses in the sample. The mail fraud and wire fraud statutes may be used to prosecute any crimes in which the postal service or other federally regulated communications system is used to defraud individuals or organizations. Mail and wire frauds generally involve attempts to trick victims – individuals, organizations or both – into purchasing goods or services that are either overpriced or nonexistent or into delivering goods or services when there is no intention to pay for them. Schemes to sell land, oil wells, and worthless bags of "rare" coins appear again and again among these offenses. These schemes generally go on for long periods and defraud large numbers of people. The amount of money involved in these cases is usually quite large. Sixty percent of the mail-fraud offenses that victimize only individuals have illegal gains of more than $100 thousand, and one in five have illegal gains of more than $1 million.

While many of the large mail frauds victimize individuals, most schemes are directed against organizations (including governments). Typically, employees victimize their own companies or agencies. In some cases the victims include both organizations and individuals. Such offenses usually occur when the offender occupies a "gatekeeper" role in the organization. The government is a victim in one of every seven of the mail fraud cases. In most of these, government employees organize the illegal action. In this sample it is rare for an outsider to victimize a private organization, and such cases generally net the smallest amount of money.

Tax fraud involves violation of the Internal Revenue Code. The code is one of the most broadly applicable criminal statutes, since every income-earning person and every organization required to withhold taxes from employees is subject to its provisions. The sample of tax fraud offenders includes people convicted of one of the three specific felony violations: willful evasion of taxes owed; failure to file required tax returns, or to record or supply information otherwise required; and making or subscribing to a document information known to be false. Most of the tax violators in the sample fail to report some or all taxable income in order to reduce the amount of taxes paid. One-fifth of the tax offenders fail to report illegal income. These individuals may be assumed to have violated other laws, and it seems likely that they were prosecuted under IRS statutes at least in part because the government was unable to prosecute them for the other offenses they had committed.

A small group of offenders reduce the taxes they claim to owe by manipulating other components of tax procedure. One method used was the inflation of the number of exemptions claimed. This approach is commonly used by "tax protesters" who claim political or religious motivations for not paying their taxes. A final subgroup are offenses in which employers fail to remit taxes lawfully withheld from employee paychecks.

Credit and lending institution fraud involves knowingly making a false statement on loan or credit applications to federally insured financial institutions. Most of the victims are banks that are members of the Federal Deposit Insurance Corporation or government agencies, such as the Department of Housing and Urban Development (HUD), that make or secure loans. Usually, fraudulent information involving the potential debtor's identity, resources, or collateral accompanies a loan application.

Approximately half of the cases in the sample involve applications for personal loans. They are usually relatively small and the offenses are quickly uncovered, either when the bank conducts an investigation before granting the loan or when the loan goes into default. Credit and lending frauds that involve business loans are less numerous in the sample, but they usually net larger amounts of money and take longer to execute than those involving personal loans. These frauds are generally larger conspiracies, and bank employees often participate. These employees rarely act without the cooperation of outsiders to victimize the organization in which they work.

False claims and statements is the criminal offense of making false claims against any federal agency or false statements in any matter involving a federal agency. False claims generally involve attempts to obtain something of value – usually cash, loans, or services (such as Medicaid) – from the government for nothing. The offenses are often organized or assisted by individuals working within the government agencies being victimized. These "gate-keepers" assure that the claim is approved despite the fact that it contains false information. Many of the false claims offenders defraud HUD. There are also many offenders prosecuted for false claims to the Veterans Administration, the Internal Revenue Service, and the Department of Health and Human Services. The false claims and statements may be made on behalf of individuals or organizations.

Appendix B: The Imprisonment Model

Table B.1. *Reduced logistic regression model used to predict the likelihood of imprisonment of the offenders in the Wheeler, Weisburd, and Bode sample*

Variable[a]	Beta	Chi Square
Intercept	−5.2	26.57
Act-related variables		
Dollar victimization	0.17	22.41
Offense complexity	0.10	4.96
Geographic spread of illegality	0.25	6.62
Maximum exposure to imprisonment	0.15	34.28
Actor-related variables		
Duncan socioeconomic index	0.01	10.69
Impeccability	−0.13	4.87
Number of prior arrests	0.09	9.64
Most serious prior arrest	0.24	5.92
Role in offense[b]		
Middle	−1.03	5.13
Minor	−0.90	11.19
Missing	−0.41	3.58
Legal process variables		
Statutory offense[c]		
Bank embezzlement	−0.34	1.49
Tax violations	0.82	9.15

Table B.1. *(cont.)*

Variable[a]	Beta	Chi Square
Mail fraud	−0.39	1.81
Securities violations	0.12	0.07
False claims and statements	−0.60	4.38
Bribery	−0.78	3.71
Antitrust	−0.94	2.00
Other variables		
Sex	−1.13	21.39
Age	0.08	3.19
Age squared	−0.001	5.01
Judicial district[d]		
Central California	0.33	1.26
Maryland	0.65	4.00
Southern New York	−0.07	0.07
Northern Texas	1.05	11.87
Northern Illinois	0.67	4.82
Western Washington	0.41	1.69

Number of Cases = 989.

Model chi-square = 305.08 with 27 degrees of freedom.

−2 log likelihood = 1058.30, $p < .001$.

[a] All variables are statistically significant at the .05 level.

[b] Major role is the excluded category.

[c] Credit fraud is the excluded category.

[d] Northern Georgia is the excluded category.

References

Adler, Freda, and William S. Laufer (eds.). 1995. "The Legacy of Anomie Theory." *Advances in Criminological Theory*, Volume 6. New Brunswick: Transaction Publishers.

Ageton, Suzanne S. 1983. *Sexual Assault among Adolescents*. Lexington: Lexington Books.

Akers, Ronald L. 1996. "Is Differential Association/Social Learning Cultural Deviance Theory?" *Criminology* **34**(2):229–247.

Akers, Ronald L. 1998. *Social Learning and Social Structure: A General Theory of Crime and Deviance*. Boston: Northeastern University Press.

Albrecht, Hans J., and Soumyo Moitra. 1988. "Escalation and Specialization: A Comparative Analysis of Patterns in Criminal Careers." In *Crime and Criminal Justice*, edited by G. Kaiser and I. Geissler, pp. 115–136. Freiburg: Max Planck Institute.

Allison, Paul D. 1984. *Event History Analysis: Regression for Longitudinal Event Data*. Beverly Hills, CA: Sage Publications.

Ambrosio, Tara-Jen, and Vincent Schiraldi. 1997. Executive Summary: From Classrooms to Cell Blocks: A National Perspective. Washington, D.C.: The Justice Policy Institute. (visited June 27, 2000). <http://www.cjcj.org/jpi/hisheredex.html>.

American Institute for Economic Research. *AIER Cost-of-Living Calculator* (visited Aug. 6, 1999). <http://aier.org/cgi-bin/colcalculator.cgi>.

Barnett, Arnold, and Anthony J. Lofaso. 1985. "Selective Incapacitation and the Philadelphia Cohort Data." *Journal of Quantitative Criminology* **1**(1):3–36.

Bartell, Ted, and L. Thomas Winfree, Jr. 1977. "Recidivist Impact of Differential Sentencing Practices for Burglary Offenders." *Criminology* **15**:387–396.

Beck, James, and Peter B. Hoffman. 1976. "Time Served and Release Performance: A Research note." *Journal of Research in Crime and Delinquency* **13**(2):127–132.

Becker, Howard S. 1963. *Outsiders: Studies in the Sociology of Deviance.* New York: Free Press of Glencoe.

Belair, Robert R. 1985. *Data Quality of Criminal History Records.* Prepared for the U.S. Department of Justice by Search Group Inc.

Bell, Daniel. 1973. *The Coming of Post-Industrial Society.* New York: Basic Books.

Benson, Michael. 1982. *Collateral Consequences of Conviction for a White Collar Crime.* Unpublished dissertation, Ann Arbor, MI: University Microfilms International.

Benson, Michael, and Francis T. Cullen. 1988. "The Special Sensitivity of White-Collar Offenders to Prison: A Critique and a Research Agenda." *Journal of Criminal Justice* **16**(3):207–215.

Benson, Michael, and Elizabeth Moore. 1992. "Are White-Collar and Common Offenders the Same? An Empirical and Theoretical Critique of a Recently Proposed General Theory of Crime." *Journal of Research in Crime and Delinquency* **29**(3):251–272.

Benson, Michael, William J. Maakestad, Francis T. Cullen, and Gilbert Geis. 1988. "District Attorneys and Corporate Crime: Surveying the Prosecutorial Gatekeepers." *Criminology* **26**(3): 505–518.

Berk, Richard A. 1987. "Causal Inference as a Prediction Problem." In *Prediction and Classification,* edited by Don M. Gottfredson and Michael Tonry, pp. 183–200. Chicago: University of Chicago Press.

Berk, Richard A., Kenneth J. Lenihan, and Peter H. Rossi. 1980. "Crime and Poverty: Some Experimental Evidence from Ex-Offenders." *American Sociological Review* **45**:766–786.

Birkbeck, Christopher. 1997. *A Profile of Offenders Entering New Mexico Prisons, 1991–1994.* Albuquerque: New Mexico Criminal and Juvenile Justice Coordinating Council.

Black, Donald. 1983. "Crime as Social Control." *American Sociological Review* **48**(1):34–45.

Blumstein, Alfred, and Jacqueline Cohen. 1978. *Estimation of Individual Crime Rates from Arrest Records.* Working Paper, Carnegie-Mellon University, Pittsburgh.

Blumstein, Alfred, Jacqueline Cohen (with Paul Hsieh). 1982. *The Duration of Adult Criminal Careers.* Final Report to the National Institute of Justice, June.

Blumstein, Alfred, and Soumyo Moitra. 1982. *Analysis of Trends in Offense Seriousness Over a Criminal Career.* Washington, D.C.: National Institute of Justice.

Blumstein, Alfred, Jacqueline Cohen, Jeffrey A. Roth, and Christy A. Visher (eds.). 1986. *Criminal Careers and "Career Criminals."* Washington, D.C.: National Academy Press.

Blumstein, Alfred, Jacqueline Cohen, and David P. Farrington. 1988. "Criminal Career Research: Its Value for Criminology." *Criminology* **26**:1–36.

Bonger, Wilelm A. 1916. *Criminality and Economic Conditions.* Boston, MA: Little, Brown.

Braithwaite, John. 1982. "Challenging Just Deserts: Punishing White-Collar Criminals." *Journal of Criminal Law and Criminology* **73**(2):723–763.

Braithwaite, John. 1985. "White Collar Crime." *Annual Review of Sociology* **11**:1–25.

Braithwaite, John. 1989. *Crime, Shame and Reintegration.* Cambridge, UK: Cambridge University Press.

Braithwaite, John, and Gilbert Geis. 1982. "On Theory and Action for Corporate Crime Control." In *On White Collar Crime*, edited by Gilbert Geis, pp. 189–210. Lexington, MA: Lexington Books.

Bridges, George S., and James A. Stone. 1986. "Effects of Criminal Punishment on Perceived Threat of Punishment: Toward an Understanding of Specific Deterrence." *Journal of Research in Crime and Delinquency* **23**(3):207–239.

Britt, Chester L. III. 1993. *Modeling Specialization and Escalation in the Criminal Career.* Washington D.C.: National Institute of Justice.

Burgess, Robert, L. 1980. "Family Violence: Implications from Evolutionary Biology." In *Understanding Crime*, edited by T. Hirschi and M. Gottfredson. Beverly Hills: Sage.

Canela-Cacho, Jose A., Alfred Blumstein and Jacqueline Cohen. 1997. "Relationship Between the Offending Frequency of Imprisoned and Free Offenders." *Criminology* **35**(1):133–175.

Clarke, Ronald V. 1980. "Situational Crime Prevention: Theory and Practice." *British Journal of Criminology* **20**(2):136–147.

Clarke, Ronald V. 1983. "Situational Crime Prevention: Its Theoretical Basis and Practical Scope. In *Crime and Justice: An Annual Review of Research*, Vol. 4, edited by Michael Tonry and Novel Morris, pp. 225–256. Chicago: University of Chicago Press.

Clarke, Ronald V. (ed.). 1992. *Situational Crime Prevention: Successful Case Studies*. Albany, NY: Harrow and Heston.

Clarke, Ronald V. 1995. "Situational Crime Prevention." In *Building a Safer Society: Strategic Approaches to Crime Prevention*, edited by Michael Tonry and David P. Farrington, pp. 91–150. Chicago: University of Chicago Press.

Clarke, Ronald V. 1999. Personal correspondence to David Weisburd.

Clarke, Ronald V., and Derek B. Cornish. 1985. "Modeling Offenders' Decisions: A Framework for Research and Policy." In *Crime and Justice: An Annual Review of Research*, edited by Michael Tonry and Norval Morris, Vol. 6, pp. 147–185. Chicago: University of Chicago Press.

Clinard, Marshall, and Peter Yeager. 1980. *Corporate Crime*. New York: Free Press.

Coffee, John. 1980. "Making the Punishment Fit the Corporation: The Problems of Finding an Optimal Corporation Criminal Sanction." *Northern Illinois University Law Review* **1**(1):3–55.

Cohen, Jacob. 1988. *Statistical Power Analysis for the Behavioral Sciences*, second edition. New York: Academic Press.

Cohen, Ben Zion, Ruth Eden, and Amnon Lazar. 1991. "The Efficacy of Probation Versus Imprisonment in Reducing Recidivism of Serious Offenders in Israel." *Journal of Criminal Justice* **19**(3): 263–270.

Coleman, James W. 1992. "The Theory of White-Collar Crime: From Sutherland to the 1990s." In *White-Collar Crime Reconsidered*, edited by Kip Schlegel and David Weisburd. Boston: Northeastern University Press.

Coleman, Stephen. 1989. *Evaluation of the Mandatory Minimum Sentence for Habitual Drunken Drivers: A Report to the Minnesota Legislature*. St. Paul: Minnesota Statistical Analysis Center.

Collins, James. 1977. *Offender Careers and Restraint: Probabilities and Policy Implications. Final draft report*. Washington, D.C.: Law Enforcement Assistance Administration, U.S. Department of Justice.

Cooper, Lynne Eickholt, Mark E. Tompkins, and Donald A. Marchand. 1979. *An Assessment of the Social Impacts of the National*

Crime Information Center and Computerized Criminal History Program. Columbia, SC: Bureau of Governmental Research and Service, University of South Carolina.

Cornish, Derek B., and Ronald V. Clarke, (eds.) 1986. *The Reasoning Criminal: Rational Choice Perspectives on Offending.* New York: Springer-Verlag.

Coser, Louis. 1967. *Continuities in the Study of Social Conflict.* New York: Free Press.

Cox, D. R., and D. Oakes. 1984. *Analysis of Survival Data.* New York: Chapman and Hall.

Cressey, D. R. 1953. *Other People's Money: A Study in the Social Psychology of Embezzlement.* Glencoe, IL: Free Press.

Cressey, D. R. 1980. "Employee Theft: The Reasons Why." *Security World* (Oct.):31–36.

Criminal Justice Information Policy. 1988, November. *Public Access to Criminal History Record Information.* NCJ-111458. Washington, D.C.: SEARCH Group, Inc.

Croall, Hazel. 1989. "Who Is the White Collar Criminal?." *British Journal of Criminology* 29(2):157–174.

Crutchfield, Robert D., and Susan R. Pitchford. 1997. "Work and Crime: The Effects of Labor Stratification." *Social Forces* 76(1):93–118.

Daly, Kathleen. 1989. "Gender and Varieties of White-Collar Crime." *Criminology* 27(4):769–794.

DeJong, Christina. 1997. "Survival Analysis and Specific Deterrence: Integrating Theoretical and Empirical Models of Recidivism." *Criminology* 35(4):561–575.

Deng, Xiaogang, and Lening Zhang. 1998. "Correlates of Self-Control: An Empirical Test of Self-Control Theory." *Journal of Crime and Justice* 21(2):89–110.

Department of Health and Human Services. 1981. User's Manual: *The National Death Index.* Hyattsville, MD: Department of Health and Human Services.

Durkheim, Emile. 1895 (1958). *The Rules of Sociological Method.* New York: The Free Press.

Durkheim, Emile. 1897 (1951). *Suicide.* Glencoe, Ill: The Free Press.

Edelhertz, Herbert. 1970. *The Nature, Impact and Prosecution of White Collar Crime.* Washington, D.C.: USGPO.

Edelhertz, Herbert, and Thomas D. Overcast, (eds.) 1982. *White Collar Crime: An Agenda for Research.* Lexington, MA: Lexington Books.

Elliott, Delbert S. 1995. "Lies, Damn Lies, and Arrest Statistics. The Sutherland Award Presentation." Presented at The American Society of Criminology Meetings in Boston.

Elliott, Delbert S., David Huizinga, and Suzanne S. Ageton. 1985. *Explaining Delinquency and Drug Use.* Beverly Hills: Sage Publications, Inc.

Elliott, Delbert S., Frankly W. Dunford, and David Huizinga. 1987. "Identification and Prediction of Career Offenders Utilizing Self-Reported and Official Data." In *Prevention of Delinquent Behavior* edited by J. D. Burchard and S. N. Burchard. Newburg Park, CA: Sage Publications.

Erikson, Kai T. 1962. "Notes on the Sociology of Deviance." *Social Problems* **9**:311.

Estrich, Susan, Mark Moore, Daniel McGillis, and William Spelman. 1983. *Dealing with Dangerous Offenders Executive Summary.* Rockville, MD: National Criminal Justice Reference Service (NCJRS).

Farrington, David P. 1986. "Age and Crime." In *Crime and Justice: An Annual Review of Research*, Vol. 7, edited by Michael Tonry and Norval Morris, pp. 189–250. Chicago: University of Chicago Press.

Farrington, David P. 1989. "Early Predictors of Adolescent Aggression and Adult Violence." *Violence and Victims* **4**(2):79–100.

Farrington, David P. 1992. "Criminal Career Research in the United Kingdom." *British Journal of Criminology* **32**(4):521–536.

Farrington, David P. 1995. "The Development of Offending and Anti-social Behaviour from Childhood: Key Findings from the Cambridge Study in Delinquent Development." *Journal of Child Psychology and Psychiatry* **36**(6):929–964.

Farrington, David P., Lloyd E. Ohlin, and James Q. Wilson. 1986. *Understanding and Controlling Crime.* New York: Springer-Verlag.

Farrington, David P., R. Loeber, D. Elliott, J. Hawkins, D. Kandel, M. Klein, J. McCord, D. Rowe, and R. Tremblay, 1988. *Final Report of the Onset Working Group Program on Human Development and Crime Behavior.* Washington, D.C.: National Institute of Justice.

Farrington, David P., and Donald J. West. 1989. *The Cambridge Study in Delinquent Development: A Long-term Followup of 411 London Males.* Cambridge, UK: Institute of Criminology, University of Cambridge.

Farrington, David P., Sandra Lambert, and Donald J. West. 1998. "Criminal Careers of Two Generations of Family Members in the

Cambridge Study in Delinquent Development." *Studies on Crime and Prevention* **7**(1):85–106.

Feeley, Malcolm. 1996. "The Decline of Women in the Criminal Process: A Comparative History" *Criminal Justice History: An International Annual* **15**:235–274.

Federal Judicial Center. 1983. *Judicial District Data Book.*

Felson, Marcus. 1998. *Crime & Everyday Life.* Thousand Oaks, CA: Pine Forge Press.

Felson, Marcus, and Ronald V. Clarke. 1998. "Opportunity Makes the Thief: Practical Theory for Crime Prevention." *Police Research Series*, Paper 98.

Fennell, Stephen A., and William N. Hall. 1980. "Due Process At Sentencing: An Empirical and Legal Analysis of the Disclosure of Presentence Reports in Federal Courts." *Harvard Law Review* **93**(8):1613–1697.

Findley, Keith A., and Meredith J. Ross. 1989. "Access, Accuracy and Fairness: The Federal Presentence Investigation Report Under *Julian* and The Sentencing Guidelines." *Wisconsin Law Review* **1989**:837–880.

Fraser, Mark, and Michael Norman. 1988. "Chronic Juvenile Delinquency and the 'Suppression Effect': An Exploratory Study." *Journal of Offender Counseling Services and Rehabilitation* **13**(1):55–73.

Gabor, Thomas. 1994. *Everybody Does It! Crime by the Public.* Toronto: University of Toronto Press.

Geis, Gilbert A. ed. 1982. *On White Collar Crime.* Lexington, MA: Lexington Books.

Geis, Gilbert A. 1992. "White-Collar Crime: What Is It?" In *White-Collar Crime Reconsidered*, edited by Kip Schlegel and David Weisburd. Boston: Northeastern University Press.

Geis, Gilbert A., and Thomas R. Clay. 1982. "Criminal Enforcement of California's Occupational Carcinogens Control Act." In *On White Collar Crime*, edited by Gilbert Geis, pp. 103–124. Lexington, MA: Lexington Books.

Gelber, Richard D., and Marvin Zelen. 1985. "Planning and Reporting of Clinical Trials." In *Medical Oncology: Basic Principles and Clinical Management of Cancer*, edited by Calabresi, Paul, Philip E. Schein, and Saul Rosenberg. New York: Macmillan.

Gilliard, Darrell K. 1999. *Prison and Jail Inmates at Midyear 1998.* Washington, D.C.: Bureau of Justice Statistics.

Glueck, Sheldon, and Eleanor Glueck. 1968. *Delinquents and Non-delinquents in Perspective.* Cambridge, MA: Harvard University Press.

Gordon, Margaret A., and Daniel Glaser. 1991. "The Use and Effects of Financial Penalties in Municipal Courts." *Criminology* **29**(4):651–676.

Gottfredson, Stephen D., and Don M. Gottfredson. 1992. *Classification, Prediction and Criminal Justice Policy.* Rockville, MD: NCJRS.

Gottfredson, Michael, and Travis Hirschi. 1988. "Science, Public, Policy and the Career Paradigm." *Criminology* **26**(1):37–55.

Gottfredson, Michael, and Travis Hirschi. 1990. *A General Theory of Crime.* Stanford, CA: Stanford University Press.

Guerry, A. M. 1833. *Essai Sur la De Statistique de la France.* Paris Crochard.

Hartung, Frank E. 1950. "White-Collar Offenses in the Wholesale Meat Industry in Detroit." *American Journal of Sociology* **56**:25–34.

Hindelang, Michael, Travis Hirschi, and Joseph Weis. 1981. *Measuring Delinquency.* Beverly Hills, CA: Sage Publications.

Hirschi, Travis. 1969. *Causes of Delinquency.* Berkeley, California: University of California Press.

Hirschi, Travis, and Michael Gottfredson. 1986. "The Distinction Between Crime and Delinquency." In *Critique and Explanation: Essays in Honor Of Gwynne Nettler,* edited by Timothy F. Hartnagel and Robert A. Silverman, pp. 55–69. New Brunswick, NJ: Transaction Books.

Hirschi, Travis, and Michael Gottfredson. 1987. "Causes of White Collar Crime." *Criminology* **25**(4):949–974.

Hopkins, Andrew. 1976. "Imprisonment and Recidivism: A Quasi-experimental Study." *Journal of Research in Crime and Delinquency* **13**(1):13–32.

Hopkins, Andrew. 1980. "Controlling Corporate Deviance." *Criminology* **18**(2):198–214.

Horney, Julie, and Ineke-Haen Marshall. 1992. "Risk Perceptions Among Serious Offenders: The Role of Crime and Punishment." *Criminology* **30**(4):575–594.

Jensen, Gary F. 1976. "Race, Achievement, and Delinquency: A Further Look at 'Delinquency in a Birth Cohort.'" *American Journal of Sociology* **82**(2):379–387.

Kandel, Denise B. 1978. *Longitudinal Research on Drug Use.* Washington, D.C.: Hemisphere Publishing Corporation.

Katz, Jack. 1979. "Legality and Equality: Plea Bargaining in the Prosecution of White-Collar and Common Crime." *Law and Society Review* 13:431–459.

Kelling, George, and Catherine M. Coles. 1996. *Fixing Broken Windows: Restoring Order and Reducing Crime in Our Communities.* New York: Free Press.

Kempf, Kimberly. 1986. "Offense Specialization Does it Exist?" In *The Reasoning Criminal,* edited by Derek, B. Cornish, and Ronald V. Clarke, pp. 186–201. New York: Springer-Verlag.

Kempf, Kimberly L. 1987. "Specialization and the Criminal Career." *Criminology* 25(2):399–420.

Kempf, Kimberly L. 1990. "Career Criminals in the 1958 Philadelphia Birth Cohort: A Follow-up of the Early Adult Years." *Criminal Justice Review.* 15(2):151–172.

Kennedy, Christopher. 1985. "Criminal Sentences for Corporations: Alternative Fining Mechanisms." *California Law Review* 73:443–482.

Kitsuse, John J. 1962. "Social Reaction to Deviant Behavior: Problems of Theory and Method." *Social Problems* 9:247–256.

Kitsuse, John J., and A. Ciciourel. 1963. "A Note on the Uses of Official Statistics." *Social Problems* 11:131–139.

Lab, Steven P. 1988. *Crime Prevention: Approaches, Practices and Evaluations.* Cincinnati: Anderson.

Labouvie, Erich. 1996. "Maturing Out of Substance Use: Selection and Self-Correction." *Journal of Drug Issues* 26(2):457–476.

Langan, Patrick, and David. P. Farrington. 1983. "Two-Track Justice? Some Evidence from an English Longitudinal Survey." *Journal of Criminal Law and Criminology* 74:519–546.

Langan, Patrick, and Lawrence A. Greenfield. 1983. *Career Patterns in Crime.* Washington D.C.: Bureau of Justice Statistics.

Levi, Michel. 1987. *Regulating Fraud: White Collar Crime and the Criminal Process.* New York: Tavistock.

Lipton, Douglas, Robert Martinson, and Judith Wilks. 1975. *The Effectiveness of Correctional Treatment: A Survey of Treatment Evaluation.* New York: Prager.

Lombroso, Casare. 1911. *Criminal Man.* Montclair, NJ: Patterson Smith.

Mak, Anita S. 1991. "Psychosocial Control Characteristics of Delinquents and Nondelinquents." *Criminal Justice and Behavior* 18(3):287–303.

Maltz, Michael D. 1984. *Recidivism*. Orlando, FL: Academic Press.

Maltz, Michael D. 1989. *Surfit: Survival Fitting and Analysis Software for Industrial, Biomedical, Correctional, and Social Science Applications.* Chicago: Michael Maltz.

Maltz, Michael D., and Richard McCleary. 1977. "The Mathematics of Behvioral Change: Recidivism and Construct Validity." *Evaluation Quarterly* 1:421–438.

Maltz, Michael D., and Richard McCleary. 1978. "Comments on 'Stability of Parameter Estimates in the Split Population Exponential Distribution." *Evaluation Quarterly* 2:650–654.

Maltz, Michael D., Richard McCleary, and Stephen M. Pollock. 1979. "Recidivism and Likelihood Functions: A Reply to Stollmack." *Evaluation Quarterly* 3:124–131.

Maltz, Michael D., and Stephen M. Pollock. 1980. "Artificial Inflation of a Delinquency Rate by a Selection Artifact." *Operations Research* 3:547–559.

Mann, Kenneth. 1985. *Defending White-Collar Crime: A Portrait of Attorneys at Work.* New Haven: Yale University Press.

Mann, Kenneth. 1992. "Procedure Rules and Information Control: Gaining Leverage over White-Collar Crime." In *White-Collar Crime Reconsidered,* edited by Kip Schlegel and David Weisburd, pp. 332–351. Boston: Northeastern University Press.

Martinson, Robert. 1974. "What Works? Questions and Answers about Prison Reform." *Public Interest* 35:22–54.

McCord, Joan. 1985. "Deterrence and the Light Touch of the Law." In *Reactions to Crime: The Public, the Police, Courts and Prisons,* edited by David Farrington and John Gunn, pp. 73–85. Chichester: John Wiley & Sons.

Meier, Robert F., and James F. Short, Jr. 1982. "Consequences of White-Collar Crime." In *White-Collar Crime,* edited by Herbert Edelhertz and Thomas D. Overcast, pp. 23–49. Lexington, MA: Lexington Books.

Merton, Robert K. 1938. "Social Structure and Anomie." *American Sociological Review* 3:672–682.

Miller, Walter B. 1958. "Lower Class Culture as a Generating Milieu of Gang Delinquency." *Journal of Social Issues* 14(3):5–19.

Morris, Norval, and Michael Tonry. 1990. *Between Prison and Probation: Intermediate Punishments in a Rational Sentencing System.* New York: Oxford University Press.

Murray, Charles A., and Louis A. Cox. 1979. *Beyond Probation: Juvenile Corrections and the Chronic Delinquent.* Beverly Hills, CA: Sage Publications.

Newcomb, Michael D. and Linda McGee. 1989. "Adolescent Alcohol Use and Other Delinquent Behaviors: A One-year Longitudinal Analysis Controlling For Sensation Seeking." *Criminal Justice and Behavior* **16**(3):345–369.

Newman, Donald. 1958. "White-Collar Crime." *Law & Contemporary Problems* **23**:735–753.

Nisan, Mordechai. 1985. "Limited Morality – A Concept and Its Educational Implications." In *Moral Education: Theory and Practice,* edited by M. Berkowitz and F. Oser, pp. 403–420. Hillsdale, NJ: Erlbaum.

Nisan, Mordechai. 1991. "The Moral Balance Model: Theory and Research Extending Our Understanding of Moral Choice and Deviation." In *Handbook of Moral Behavior and Development* Vol. 3, edited by W. Kurtines and J. Gewirtz. Hillsdale, NJ: Erlbaum.

Nisan, Mordechai and Gaby Horenczyk. 1990. "Moral Balance: The Effect of Prior Behavior on Decision in Moral Conflict." *British Journal of Social Psychology* **29**:29–42.

Osborn, S. G., and D. J. West. 1978. "The Effectiveness of Various Predictors of Criminal Careers." *Journal of Adolescence* **1**(2):101–117.

Passas, Nikos, and Robert Agnew (eds.). 1997. *The Future of Anomie Theory.* Boston: Northeastern University Press.

Perin, Constance. 1977. *Everything in Its Place: Social Order and Land Use in America.* Princeton, NJ: Princeton University Press.

Petersilia, Joan. 1980. "Criminal Career Research: A Review of Recent Evidence." In *Crime and Justice: An Annual Review of Research* Vol. 2, edited by Norval Morris and Michel Torny, pp. 321–379. Chicago: University of Chicago.

Petersilia, Joan, and Susan Turner. 1986. *Prison Versus Probation in California.* Santa Monica, CA: The Rand Corporation.

Polk, K., C. Alder, G. Bazemore, G. Black, S. Cordray, G. Coventry, J. Galvin, and M. Temple. 1981. *Becoming Adult: An Analysis of Maturational Development from Age 16 to 30 of a Cohort of Young Men.* Final Report of the Marion Country Youth Study. Eugene, OR: University of Oregon.

Posner, Richard A. 1980. "Optimal Sentences for White Collar Criminals." *American Law Review* **17**(4):409–418.

Poyner, Bary. 1993. "What Works in Crime Prevention: An Overview of Evaluations." In *Crime Prevention Studies* Vol. 1, edited by Ronald V. Clarke, pp. 7–34. Monsey: Criminal Justice Press.

Quetelet, A. 1835. *Sur l'Homme et le Developpement de ses Facultes, ou Essai de Physique Sociale.* Paris: Bachelier.

Quinney, Earl. 1963. "Occupational Structure and Criminal Behavior: Prescription Violation by Retail Pharmacists." *Social Problems* **11**:179–185.

Rand Corperation. 1985. *Criminal Justice at Rand.* Rand Corperation Institute for Civil Justice.

Reiss, Albert J., and Albert Biderman. 1980. *Data Sources on White-Collar Law Breaking.* Washington, D.C.: USGPO.

Reiss, Albert J., and Michael. Tonry (eds.). 1986. *Communities and Crime.* Chicago University Press.

Rodriguez, Orlando, and David Weisburd. 1991. "The Integrated Social Control Model and Ethnicity: The Case of Puerto Rican American Delinquency." *Criminal Justice and Behavior* **18**(4):464–479.

Ross, E. A. 1907. *Sin and Society: An Analysis of Latter-Day Iniquity.* Boston: Houghton Mifflin.

Rossi, Peter H., Richard A. Berk, and Kenneth J. Lenihan. 1980. *Money, Work, and Crime: Experimental Evidence.* New York: Academic Press.

Sampson, Robert J. 1987. "Urban Black Violence: The Effect of Male Joblessness and Family Disruption." *American Journal of Sociology* **93**(2):348–382.

Sampson, Robert J., and John J. Laub. 1990. "Crime and Deviance over the Life Course: The Salience of Adult Social Bonds." *American Sociological Review* **55**(5):609–627.

Sampson, Robert J., and John J. Laub. 1992. "Crime and Deviance in the Life Course." *Annual Review of Sociology* **18**:63–84.

Sampson, Robert J., and John J. Laub. 1993. *Crime in the Making: Pathways and Turning Points Through Life.* Cambridge, MA: Harvard University Press.

Sampson, Robert J., and John J. Laub. 1995. "Understanding Variability in Lives Through Time: Contributions of Life Course Criminology." *Studies on Crime and Crime Prevention* **4**(2):143–158.

Sapp, Allen D. 1989. "Arrest for Major Crimes: Tends and Patterns for Elderly Offenders." *Older Offenders: Current Trends.* New York: The Haworth Press.

SAS Institute. 1990. *SAS/STAT Users Guide,* Version 6, fourth edition, Vol. 2. Cary, NC: SAS Institute.

Schlegel, Kip, and David Weisburd (eds.). 1992. *White-Collar Crime Reconsidered.* Boston: Northeastern University Press.

Schmidt, Peter, and Ann Dryden Witte. 1984. *An Economic Analysis of Crime and Justice: Theory, Methods and Applications.* Orlando, FL: Academic Press.

Schmidt, Peter, and Ann Dryden Witte. 1988. *Predicting Recidivism Using Survival Models.* New York: Springer-Verlag.

Schulke, Beverly Brown. 1993. *Women and Criminal Recidivism: A Study of Social Constraints.* Ann Arbor, MI: University Microfilms International.

Sechrest, Lee, White O. Susan, and Elizabeth D. Brown. 1979. *The Rehabilitation of Criminal Offenders: Problems and Prospects.* Washington, D.C.: National Academy of Sciences.

Shapiro, Susan P. 1981. *Thinking About White Collar Crime: Matters of Conceptualization and Research.* Washington, D.C.: National Institute of Justice.

Shapiro, Susan P. 1984. *Wayward Capitalists: Targets of the Securities and Exchange Commission.* New Haven, CT: Yale University Press.

Shapiro, Susan P. 1985. "The Road Not Taken: The Elusive Path to Criminal Prosecution for White Collar Offenders." *Law & Society Review* **19**:179–217.

Shapiro, Susan P. 1990. "Collaring the Crime, Not the Criminal: 'Liberating' the Concept of White-Collar Crime." *American Sociological Review* **93**:623–658.

Shaw, Clifford R. 1929. *Delinquency Areas.* Chicago: University of Chicago Press.

Shaw, Clifford R., and Henry D. McKay. 1931. Social Factors in Juvenile Delinquency. *Report on the Causes of Crime,* Vol. 2. Washington, D.C.: National Commission on Law Observance and Enforcement.

Shaw, Clifford R., and Henry D. McKay. 1942. *Juvenile Delinquency and Urban Areas.* Chicago: University of Chicago Press.

Sherman, Lawrence W., Patrick Gartin, David Doi, and Susan Miler. 1986. *The Effects of Jail Time on Drunk Drivers.* Presentation to the American Society of Criminology, Atlanta, GA, November.

Shichor, David. 1997. "Three Strikes as a Public Policy: The Convergence of the New Penology and the McDonaldization of Punishment." *Crime and Delinquency* **43**(4):470–492.

Short, James F., and F. Ivan Nye. 1958. "Extent of Unrecorded Juvenile Delinquency, Tentative Conclusions." *Journal of Criminal Law, Criminology, and Police Science* **49**:296–302.

Shover, Neal. 1983. *Age and Changing Criminal Behavior of Ordinary Property Offenders.* Rockville, MD: National Criminal Justice Reference Center.

Shover, Neal. June 4, 1999. Personal correspondence to David Weisburd.

Simpson, Sally S., and Christopher S. Koper. 1992. "Deterring Corporate Crime." *Criminology* **30**(3):347–375.

Simmel, Georg. 1964. *Conflict and the Web of Group Affiliations.* New York: Free Press.

Sims, Barbara, and Mark Jones. 1997. "Predicting Success or Failure on Probation: Factors Associated with Felony Probation Outcomes." *Crime and Delinquency* **43**(3):314–327.

Sinclair, Upton. 1906. *The Jungle.* New York: Doubleday, Page.

Stattin, Hakan, David Magnusson, and Howard Reichel. 1989. "Criminal Activity at Different Ages: A Study Based on a Swedish Longitudinal Research Population." *British Journal of Criminology* **29**(4):368–385.

Steffens, Lincoln. 1903. *The Struggle for Self-Government: Being an Attempt to Trace American Political Corruption to Its Sources in Six States of the United States.* New York: Phillips McClure.

Stotland, Ezra, Michael Brintnall, Andre L'Heureux, and Eva Ashmore. 1980. "Do Convictions Deter Home Repair Fraud?" In *White Collar Crime: Theory and Research,* edited by Gilbert Geis and Ezra Stotland, pp. 252–265. Beverly Hills: Sage Publications.

Sutherland, Edwin. 1939. *Principles of Criminology.* Chicago: J. B. Lippincott.

Sutherland, Edwin H. 1940. "White Collar Criminality." *American Sociological Review* **5**:1–12.

Sutherland, Edwin H. 1945. Is White Collar a Crime? *American Sociological Review* **10**:132–139.

Sutherland, Edwin H. 1949. *White Collar Crime.* New York: Dryden Press.

Sutherland, Edwin H., and Donald R. Cressey. 1960. *The Principles of Criminology.* Chicago: J. B. Lippincott.

Sviridoff, Michele, and Jerome E. McElroy. 1985. *Employment and Crime: A Summary Report.* New York: Vera Institute of Justice.

Sykes, Gresham M., and David Matza. 1957. "Techniques of Neutralization: A Theory of Delinquency." *American Sociological Review* **22**:664–670.

Thrasher, Frederic. 1927. *The Gang.* Chicago: University of Chicago Press.

Tillman, Robert. 1987. "The Size of the 'Criminal Population': The Prevalence and Incidence of Adult Arrests." *Criminology* **25**(3):561–579.

Tittle, Charles R. 1988. "Two Empirical Regularities (Maybe) in Search of an Explanation: Commentary on the Age/Crime Debate." *Criminology* **26**:75–85.

Tracy, Paul E., and Kimberly Kempf-Leonard. 1996. *Continuity and Discontinuity in Criminal Careers.* New York: Plenum Press.

Tracy, Paul E., Marvin E. Wolfgang, and Robert M. Figlio. 1985. *Delinquency in Two Birth Cohorts: Executive Summary.* Washington, D.C.: National Institute of Juvenile Justice and Delinquency Prevention.

United States Bureau of Census. 1977. *Statistical Abstracts of the United States.* Washington, D.C.: U.S. Bureau of Census.

United States Sentencing Commission. 1987. *Sentencing Guidelines and Policy Statements.* Washington, D.C.: U.S. Government Printing Office.

United States Sentencing Commission. 1991. "The Federal Sentencing Guidelines: A Report on the Operation of the Guidelines System and Short-Term Impacts on Disparity in Sentencing, Use of Incarceration, and Prosecutorial Discretion and Plea Bargaining." Washington, D.C.: U.S. Sentencing Commission.

Vera Institute of Justice. 1977. *Felony Arrests: Their Prosecution and Disposition in New York City's Courts.* New York: Vera Institute of Justice.

Visher, Christy A., Pamela K. Lattimore, and Richard L. Linster. 1991. "Predicting the Recidivism of Serious Youthful Offenders Using Survival Models." *Criminology* **29**(3):329–366.

Visher, Christy A., and Jeffery A. Roth. 1986. "Participation in Criminal Careers." In *Criminal Careers and Career Criminals,* edited by A. Blumstein, J. Cohen, J. Roth, and C. Visher. Washington, D.C.: National Academy Press.

Vitiello, Michael. 1997. "Three Strikes: Can We Return To Rationality?." *Journal of Criminal Law and Criminology* **87**(2):395–481.

Wallerstein, J. A., and C. E. Wyle. 1947. "Our Law-Abiding Law-Breakers." *Probation* **25**:107–112.

Waring, Elin J. 1993. *Co-offending in White Collar Crime: A Network Approach.* Ann Arbor, MI: University of Microfilms International.

Waring, Elin, and Gisela Bichler. 1997. "Criminal Careers as Sequences: An Exploratory Analysis of Criminal Histories in a Sample of White Collar Offenders." American Sociological Association, August 1997.

Waring, Elin, David Weisburd, and Ellen Chayet. 1995. "White Collar Crime and Anomie." *Advances in Criminological Theory,* **6**:207–225.

Warr, Mark. 1998. "Life-Course Transitions and Desistance from Crime." *Criminology* **36**(2):183–216.

Watkins, John C., Jr. 1977. "White-Collar Crime, Legal Sanctions and Social Control." *Crime & Delinquency* **23**(3):290–303.

Weisberg, Jacob. "The Way We Live Now: 8-15-99; Body Count." *New York Times Magazine.* August 15, 1999, at 17.

Weisburd, David. 1997. *Reorienting Crime Prevention Research and Policy: From the Causes of Criminality to the Context of Crime.* Washington, D.C.: National Institute of Justice.

Weisburd, David. 1998. *Statistics in Criminal Justice.* Belmont, CA: West/Wadsworth Publishing Company.

Weisburd, David (with Anthony Petrosino and Gail Mason). 1993. "Design Sensitivity in Criminal Justice Experiments." *Crime and Justice* **17**:337–379.

Weisburd, David, Ellen F. Chayet, and Elin Waring. 1990. "White-Collar Crime and Criminal Careers: Some Preliminary Findings." *Crime & Delinquency* **3**:342–355.

Weisburd, David, Stanton Wheeler, Elin Waring, and Nancy Bode. 1991. *Crimes of the Middle Classes.* New Haven, CT: Yale University Press.

Weisburd, David, Elin Waring, and Ellen Chayet. 1995. "Specific Deterrence in a Sample of Offenders Convicted of White-Collar Crimes." *Criminology* **33**(4):587–607.

Weisburd, David, and Tom McEwen. 1998. *Crime Mapping & Crime Prevention. Crime Prevention Studies,* Vol. 8. Monsey, NY: Crimal Justice Press.

Weisburd, David, Elin Waring, and Ellen Chayet. 2000. *Study of White-Collar Crime and Criminal Careers.* National Archives of Criminal Justice Data. The Inter-University Consortium for Political and Social Research. Ann Arbor: University of Michigan.

West, Donald, and David Farrington. 1973. *Who Becomes Delinquent?* London: Heinemann.

Wheeler, Stanton. 1967. "Criminal Statistics: A Reformulation of the Problem." *Journal of Criminal Law and Criminology and Police Science* **58**:317–324.

Wheeler, Stanton. 1983. "White Collar Crime: History of an Idea." *Encyclopedia of Crime and Justice*, pp. 1652–1656. New York: Free Press.

Wheeler, Stanton, Kenneth Mann, and Austin Sarat. 1988. *Sitting in Judgment: The Sentencing of White Collar Offenders.* New Haven, CT: Yale University Press.

Wheeler, Stanton, and Mitchell Lewis Rothman. 1982. "The Organization as Weapon in White Collar Crime." *Michigan Law Review* **80**:1403–1426.

Wheeler, Stanton, David Weisburd, and Nancy Bode. 1982. "Sentencing the White Collar Offender: Rhetoric and Reality." *American Sociological Review* **47**(5):641–659.

Wheeler, Stanton, David Weisburd, and Nancy Bode. 1988. *Study of Convicted Federal White-Collar Crime Defendants.* National Archives of Criminal Justice Data. The Inter-University Consortium for Political and Social Research. Ann Arbor: University of Michigan.

Wheeler, Stanton, David Weisburd, Elin Waring, and Nancy Bode. 1988. "White Collar Crimes and Criminals." *American Criminal Law Review* **25**(3):331–358.

Wilkins, Leslie T. 1965. *Social Deviance: Social Policy, Action, and Research.* Englewood Cliffs, N.J.: Prentice-Hall.

Wilson, James Q., and Richard J. Herrnstein. 1985. *Crime & Human Nature.* New York: Simon and Schuster.

Wolfgang, Marvin E., R. M. Figlio, and Thorsten Sellin. 1972. *Delinquency in a Birth Cohort.* Chicago: University of Chicago Press.

Wolfgang, Marvin E., Robert M. Figlio, Paul E. Tracy, and Simon I. Singer. 1985. *The National Survey of Crime Severity.* Washington, D.C.: Department of Justice.

Wolfgang, Marvin E., Terence P. Thornberry, and Robert M. Figlio. 1987. *From Boy to Man, from Delinquency to Crime.* Chicago: University of Chicago Press.

Yale Law Journal. 1982. "A Proposal to Ensure Accuracy in Presentence Investigation Reports." *The Yale Law Journal* **91**:1225–1249.

Zietz, Dorothy. 1981. *Women Who Embezzle or Defraud: A Study of Convicted Felons.* New York: Praeger Publishers.

Zimring, Franklin E., and Gordon J. Hawkins. 1973. *Deterrence: The Legal Threat in Crime Control.* Chicago: University of Chicago Press.

Index

183